BIRTH
OF THE
LIGHT BODY

An inspirational treatise by

NADA-YOLANDA

With medical data by

ROBERT H. KNAPP, M.D.

MARK-AGE
⑦
LOVE IN ACTION

MARK-AGE
Fort Lauderdale, Florida, USA

Song lyrics from *I Am Golden Light* reprinted by permission.
© 1990 by Deborah Jacobs and Janet Thiemermann

Price: $23.00

ISBN 0-912322-07-1
Library of Congress Catalog Card Number: 94-78199

FIRST EDITION

Manufactured in the United States of America
by Quebecor Printing, Inc., Kingsport, Tennessee

CONTENTS

MEDICAL GUIDELINE

Throughout this book, a holistic approach is recommended for healing any mental, emotional, soul or physical disorder. This includes the services of licensed healers in all aspects of medicine. Nothing given in this book should be interpreted as a substitute for proper medical treatment. See a physician when you have questions about any aspect of your health or when you need medical care. Use this book's information about the twelve spiritual qualities in conjunction with the most effective methods that modern medicine has to offer.

ILLUSTRATIONS
Charts & Figures

BIRTH
OF THE
LIGHT BODY

Before Your Birth

Conception: *In the Beginning*

Gestation: *Development of Treatise*

Labor: *Begin Your Birth*

CONCEPTION
In the Beginning

From the beginning of my spiritual awakening and development in 1956, the ascended masters told me I was to learn how to become a master teacher on the Earth. Step by step, in an organized and disciplined way, they prepared me to bring forth my light body, the resurrected form innate to each immortal child of God.

Although many spiritual teachers throughout history have demonstrated the light body—also termed the immortal, incorruptible, electric, fourth dimensional, etheric or Christ body—none has demonstrated it as completely or as powerfully as our planetary way shower, Sananda, who last incarnated on Earth as Jesus the Christ of Nazareth. "Whoever believes in me," he said, "will perform the same works as I do myself, and will perform even greater works, because I am going to the Father." His resurrection and ascension into the light body paved the way for our own demonstrations, both as individual light workers and as a collective force to prepare the planet for the New Age of Aquarius.

Actually, it is the *rebirth* of the light body on Earth. For mankind had manifested his Christ body on Earth prior to his final fall into physical, third dimensional matter twenty-six million years ago. We are reevolving into our original state of I Am or Christ or cosmic consciousness in these Latter Days. This is the harvest time, the purification period, the Mark Age: the age of marks or signs of the times that herald the arrival of spiritual cleansing, fulfillment and graduation for each soul. We are closing out the forty-year cycle of transition, begun in 1960, to bring planet Earth into the Golden Era of peace, love and brotherhood.

Prior to Sananda's Second Coming in his light body as Jesus of Nazareth around the year 2000, we are to redemonstrate how beings of light in a fourth dimensional consciousness operate in a rapidly changing three-dimensional world. This is the other meaning of the Second Coming: our coming again, or return, to Christ awareness.

In my role as a teacher, birthing the light body of the I Am Self is the goal and mission of my soul evolution. But my spiritual rebirth also serves as an example for the whole race of man, as every human being eventually must achieve this same reanchoring of I Am consciousness on Earth. Thus my demonstration, building upon those of many teachers before me, is but a catalyst for your own rebirth.

3

NADA-YOLANDA
In front of my soul portrait, "The Carpenter's Child"

Via automatic writing, my master teachers—Sananda/Jesus, Mary the mother, Paul the Apostle, and others—already had channeled information to me about my role and mission before I had met Mark/Charles Boyd Gentzel, with whom I cofounded the Mark-Age organization on February 21, 1960, in Miami, Florida. Prior to my meeting and working with Mark, I had been interested predominantly in psychology, philosophy and parapsychology. As a developing channel, I had been totally absorbed in my own psychic and spiritual development. But my spiritual partnership with Mark expanded my horizons exponentially.

Mark, himself a metaphysician and author, introduced me to his writings and those of other highly respected teachers. I discovered that many of their inspirations dovetailed with the cosmic lessons the ascended masters were channeling through me. Among these gifted thinkers was Charles Fillmore, who, with his wife Myrtle in 1889, had cofounded Unity School of Christianity. In his high Self or I Am level, Charles Fillmore is the master teacher Hilarion. On the Hierarchal Board, or spiritual government of our solar system, he is Chohan or Director of the Fifth Ray of Unity, Integration and Healing. Significantly, one of his past incarnations was as Paul, apostle to Christ Jesus of Nazareth.

Since his ascension two thousand years ago, Jesus has prepared humanity for evolution back into the light body. He has directed a plan

4

and a program whereby the ascended masters of the Hierarchal Board gradually have released more comprehensive teachings on the birth of the light body. Thus, Jesus revealed the first basic outline of this knowledge to his apostle, Charles Fillmore, who wrote *The Twelve Powers of Man* in 1930. (See also Fillmore's *Metaphysical Bible Dictionary*.)

The basic premise is that there are twelve divine characteristics of the Christ or I Am Self. Metaphysically, these spiritual qualities are symbolized by the twelve apostles of Christ Jesus, and they outpicture as the twelve major systems of the physical body (see chart on page 10). Each spiritual initiate must refine and eventually master each of the twelve characteristics in order to manifest fully Christ consciousness on Earth.

It was upon this solid foundation, initially cemented by Fillmore, that Sananda/Jesus continued to build when he inspired me to develop the current treatise, *Birth of the Light Body.*

GESTATION
Development of Treatise

In 1975, Sananda informed me that after nineteen years of intensive spiritual training and dedication, I had completed the preparation for the birth of the light body on Earth. Moreover, the time was ripe for an awakening humanity to take full advantage of deeper teachings, in order to cooperate consciously with the birth of the light body prior to the Second Coming. The Master indicated he was ready to expand upon and to refine the revelation Fillmore had received; and, in conjunction with Hilarion, would inspire updated medical information.

One significant change, for example, involved the correct order of the twelve spiritual characteristics/disciples. Despite what had been recorded in scriptures, Sananda relayed, this was the true order in which he, as Jesus of Nazareth, had called the twelve apostles. Each individual must anchor and birth the twelve qualities in this same sequence.

Charles Fillmore had achieved a spiritual breakthrough for the ages. Yet, he lacked the advantage of modern medicine and psychiatry to be able to expound fully on the birth of the light body through the mortal vessel. Scientifically, as well as spiritually, the time had not been ripe.

Quickly, though, the Master desired to expedite the hierarchal plan through Mark-Age. On our staff we had a medical doctor with psychiatric training, Robert H. Knapp, M.D. Having graduated from Upstate Medical School of the State University of New York in Syracuse in

ROBERT H. KNAPP, M.D.

1972, he had taken one year of residency there in psychiatry and then had practiced holistic medicine for one year. He had joined our staff in 1974 as director of our Healing Haven division. Therefore, the masters assigned Dr. Robert to witness, record, verify and explain the glorious guidance of Jesus the Christ through me.

In a six-week period from July into September of 1975, in almost daily communion with Sananda/Jesus, I received this treatise inspirationally, not via mental telepathic communication. Throughout this exhilarating, revelatory period, Dr. Robert worked with me to monitor my psychic and physical experiences and to verify medical data that I intuned psychically.

Initial research to confirm this treatise took four months. Add to that the ensuing twenty years, bringing us to today. With the assistance of dozens of staff and associates, we have continued to test and to verify— actually to live and to prove to ourselves—that this system of light-body birthing works. Based on the living laboratory of our personal experience, we are satisfied that you, too, can achieve lasting results when you apply this system to birth your light body on Earth.

LABOR
Begin Your Birth

Each person is a child of God. Inherently each person is a Christ, evolving to full knowledge and expression of co-creative powers with our Father-Mother Creator. Each one has a unique, specialized, irreplaceable role in the whole equation of the Son of God, or entire Christ body, which is mankind throughout the universe.

The twelve spiritual characteristics exist full-blown within the I Am consciousness of each of us. It is not a matter of creating them; it is a matter of birthing them, anchoring them, refining them through all levels of our mortal being: mind, body and soul. This treatise, therefore, is a guidebook to your personal I Am Self discovery.

To provide a format easy for study, I have divided each chapter into four categories: Metaphysical Interpretation, Physical Data, Color Visualization, and Song Inspiration.

Metaphysical Interpretation. This section presents the inspirations I received for each characteristic and corresponding disciple while I was in the high Self state in communion with Sananda/Jesus. Each chapter is designed to be a springboard for your own meditations, a doorway by which you may enter the living laboratory of your consciousness.

Physical Data. Written by Robert H. Knapp, M.D., this section is intended to give the layperson an overview of each physical system, based on the latest medical research. The data are supplemented by basic medical drawings, also by Dr. Robert.

Color Visualization. For each of the twelve characteristics there is a corresponding color, for which I also received a visualization. Use these in your meditations as tools to anchor and refine the characteristics.

Song Inspiration. This section, designed to evoke poetic inspiration, comprises the lyrics of songs written by longtime Mark-Age members Deborah Jacobs and Janet Thiemermann, both of Austin, Texas. In the mid-to-late 1980s, upon study of the initial draft of this manuscript, Deborah and Janet were inspired to write a song for each of the twelve characteristics, plus one to evoke the I Am, light body.

Two other musicians, Achim Thiemermann and Doug Seiter, joined Deborah and Janet to produce a professional music tape, entitled *I Am Golden Light*, released in July 1990. This inspiring cassette brings the spiritually-enhancing power of sound to aid you in uplifting each divine characteristic and its corresponding chakra center and physical system. (See ad at back of book.)

•

Finally, before you begin your birth, review a few basic concepts that will help you understand this treatise. Other terms may be found in the Glossary. For your additional study, Mark-Age has published a wealth of inspirational and channeled material on the light body, the I Am Self, the Latter Days, and the Second Coming. (See ad at back of book.)

I Am Nation. Each light worker is responsible to birth his or her I Am consciousness and light-body powers on Earth. But no one is separate from the whole. We each are interrelated with one another, and our rebirth of I Am consciousness must serve the overall good of the whole.

7

Unified in our spiritual demonstrations, we form the I Am Nation: the congregation of all souls on Earth who dedicate themselves to serve God, first and foremost, and the I Am Self of each other one.

Each person is a potential I Am Nation citizen, regardless of race, gender, age, nationality, religion or esoteric group affiliation. As light workers united to birth the light body, we are demonstrating the prototype of spiritual government to come on Earth, to be inaugurated by Sananda/Jesus after his Second Coming around the year 2000.

As in the macrocosm of planetary life, so in the microcosm of individual consciousness: each of us reflects the I Am Nation within oneself. Our I Am Nation citizens/cells are those thoughts and patterns in our consciousness and lower bodies that make up the total I Am Self as incarnated in our individual soul and personality. Thus, as we purify our own body/temple/nation within, we contribute to the collective demonstration of all I Am Selves who are implanting the I Am Nation on Earth. As we raise ourselves into light-body consciousness, so we raise planet Earth into the fourth dimension.

Aura. The force field of energy around an individual is termed the aura. The auric field is composed of the astral, mental and emotional bodies. The astral body is similar in shape and appearance to the physical body, but is composed of more-refined energy that is visible only to one's psychic senses. (Some occult schools refer to the astral body as the etheric double; but we use the term *etheric* to refer to the Christ or electric or light body.) The mental and emotional bodies are matrices or force fields of one's thoughts and feelings.

Bodies of Man. Each person has seven major, interrelated bodies. Each body expresses at a different frequency vibration and has a different function. They are: physical, astral, mental, emotional, etheric, God consciousness, and one not yet revealed. The first four are known as the lower, the last three as the higher, bodies. By refining and aligning the four lower bodies with the etheric or light body, we provide the necessary force field by which to birth or anchor our light body on Earth.

Chakras. A chakra is a center of energy focus in one's body. There are seven spiritual centers in the light body, seven corresponding chakras in the astral body, and seven corresponding endocrine glands in the physical body. The seven major chakras are: crown, third eye, throat, heart, solar plexus, regenerative, and sacral. (See chart on page 10 for correlation of chakras with the twelve characteristics.)

8

Involution/Evolution. The twelve characteristics may be divided into six pairs of dual polarities. Each pair is comprised of one quality that operates on the positive-active-male principle, and one that operates on the negative-receptive-female principle. For example, the first pair comprises faith, a positive polarity, and strength, a negative polarity.

The first six characteristics represent spiritual, immortal man (Son of God) involuting or descending into the physical plane. Symbolically, these three pairs signify the points of a downward-pointing triangle. The second six characteristics also comprise three pairs, which signify the points of an upward-pointing triangle; they represent physical or mortal man (son of man) evolving back to I Am consciousness. Together, the two interlocking triangles compose the cosmic symbol of the six-pointed Star of David. (See Figure A.)

As symbolized by the Star of David, one must express complete equipoise of all twelve characteristics (balanced positive-negative polarities) in order to birth the light body on Earth.

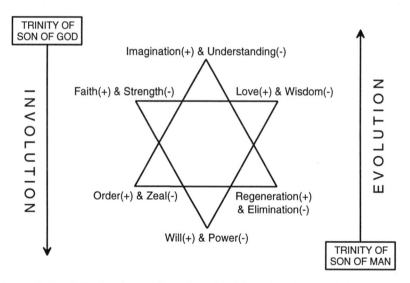

Figure A. Involution/evolution: Star of David with twelve characteristics.

Begin now the labor to birth your light body. Lovingly nurture your new birth, or rebirth, of I Am consciousness. Spirit awaits your diligent application of Its divine system. Your light body, in resurrected glory, is ready to manifest on Earth. *Behold, your birth has begun! Hail to the Christ in thee!*

Twelve Spiritual Powers of I Am Self

POWER	PHYSICAL	CHAKRA	DISCIPLE	COLOR
1. Faith	Cerebrum of brain	Crown	Simon Peter	Royal blue
2. Strength	Spinal cord & nerves	Spine as conduit	Andrew	Lemon yellow
3. Love	Heart & circulatory system	Heart	John	White
4. Wisdom	Pituitary & endocrine system	Third Eye	James son of Zebedee	Green
5. Will	Respiratory system	Throat	Matthew	Sky blue
6. Power	Larynx, muscles & limbs	Throat	Philip	Deep aqua
7. Imagination	Thalamus & psychic senses (ESP)	Third Eye	Nathanael Bartholomew	Crystal clear
8. Understanding	Five senses & analytical aspects	Five minor centers	Thomas	Cream yellow
9. Order	Digestive system, bones & skin	Solar Plexus	James son of Alphaeus	Mustard yellow
10. Zeal	Hypothalamus & medulla oblongata	Third Eye	Simon the Cananaean	Rosy pink
11. Regeneration	Reproductive system	Regenerative	Judas Iscariot	Ruby red
12. Elimination	Urinary system & colon	Sacral	Jude Thaddaeus	Violet
LIGHT BODY		I AM SELF		GOLD

1. Faith

Metaphysical Interpretation: *Simon Peter*

Physical Data: *Cerebrum of Brain*

Color Visualization: *Royal Blue*

Song Inspiration: *Faith*

METAPHYSICAL INTERPRETATION
Simon Peter

As children of God, we are spirit, light, the Son part of the Trinity of Father-Mother-Son. Our eternal and indestructible vessel for this spiritual, I Am Self part of our being is the light body. As we involuted into third dimensional frequency, falling into Earth plane matter, the soul formed an astral body. This body contains a memory bank, an akashic record to store our experiences. In the soul, the record keeper, are encapsulated our prior thoughts, experiences, feelings, actions, patterns of reactions.

When we manifest in a physical body on Earth, the cerebrum of the brain is the apparatus which receives this information from the soul record, to influence our Earth plane freewill decisions and to carry out our physical functions. Our cerebrum also relays information—gathered from various experiences during our current incarnation—to the soul body. We can liken the cerebrum to a wondrous computer and the soul record to a collection of data on disks. Thus we can understand that the cerebrum is not the soul record or memory, but rather an instrument to gain access to the data stored in the soul, as well as to enter new information there. Both the cerebrum of the brain and the soul record are separate units or functions, and they need each other to permit proper and full functioning of the soul within the physical vessel.

Especially with its protective covering of the skull, the cerebrum is like a rock. "Upon this rock, I will build," says the Christ. Into this uppermost section of the brain, the central computer, the soul relays information about past experiences, adventures, thoughts and feelings throughout the cosmos. If there has been misuse or abuse of one of the body or soul systems, the information is stored in this computer. Likewise, all the good, positive and constructive aspects of our soul experiences are recorded there.

Therefore, in evolving back to the light body, we should retain only those programs which are cosmically correct. From the cerebrum, we erase what has been of the negative and restore programs which are positive, creative and constructive. From our I Am level of consciousness, through the conscious or analytical mind via the subconscious or soul-memory recall, we must deliberately and consciously impregnate each of the twelve divine characteristics designed to serve the Christ or

I Am Self. The cerebrum, as well as the corresponding crown chakra, must be activated for the anointed state of being to manifest through the physical body.

Both metaphysically and physically, the crown chakra/cerebrum—which relates to the faith characteristic of the spiritual Self—is the control center for involution and evolution. It represents the first step of the Father/idea, our thinking process, which creates the patterns for all levels and expressions of both our physical-body and light-body developments.

Jesus of Nazareth is the Christ pattern for Earthman's evolution from physical, third dimensional form into the fourth dimensional, light-body form of the I Am Self. He said to his first chosen apostle, Simon, "You are Peter, the rock upon which I will build my church." Here he announced at the outset that Simon, the mortal son of man, would be transformed into Peter, the immortal son of God. This transmutation would be done via the cerebrum computer, the rock upon which the light body (church) is to be built. The cornerstone of the light body consists of unequivocal reliance on, and total trust and faith in, God.

Simon represents the hearing of the first word, the divine sound *Om. Sss-I Am-Om.* This vibration transmutes and solidifies into our consciousness and becomes the rock upon which we can build faith in the divine laws of God: the Lord, the I Am; Yahweh, as the Old Testament prophets called our Father or I Am Self. As we hear each sound or word of divine truth, we record it in the soul data bank via the cerebrum. Truth becomes the law which governs our new cells in reaching for the I Am or Christ state of consciousness.

All form is built on a trinity principle: Father-Mother-Son. In the involution into matter (Son of God as an inverted triangle) and the evolution of matter back into original spiritual state (son of man as an upright triangle), we have the interlocking, six-pointed Star of David, the symbol of our immortal-mortal existence on Earth. The twelve divine characteristics are six partners, active and receptive polarities (see page 9). In the first step toward reevolution into I Am Self action, Peter/faith/cerebrum is the primary, positive, active principle. His brother, Andrew/strength/spinal cord and nerves, is the receiver or the receptive partner. As a pair, they represent the first principle of the Son of God involuting into matter: Father/thought and mental functioning.

Jesus, representing our I Am Self, told Peter, "You will have the keys to the kingdom." The keys are the faith that unlocks the thoughts about our divine heritage and powers as a son of God. It is through our faith that we discover those other eleven characteristics which comprise our physical-body systems, our mental attitudes, our emotional reactions and equipment necessary to put feeling and love into our actions; plus, our soul memories of past experiences throughout our immortal existence.

Through total trust in God and His just laws and systems, we reprogram—via our central computer, the cerebrum—new physical, mental, emotional and soul functions. It is absolutely necessary to take time, to use the requisite energy, to be persevering in nature—regardless of any obstacles of mind, body or soul memories—to build slowly and surely upon this rock of faith. Everything we think, remember, experience mentally, emotionally, psychically and physically is programed via the cerebrum of the brain.

That is why the first essential aspect of the Christ consciousness to be called forth must be faith: faith in and *of* God and His divine laws; faith that His will and timing are always for our highest good. In faith we therefore proclaim, "Thy will be done through my present instrument or vehicle." Regardless of how impatient we are to progress and how much we intellectually desire to accept divine will, we cannot receive the other eleven spiritual characteristics until we have anchored firmly and permanently this primary one, faith, into every thought, word and activity. Where faith in and of God is concerned, there is nothing too small or too great to be overlooked.

Jesus told Peter, "Whatsoever you shall bind on Earth shall be bound in heaven. And whatsoever you shall loosen on Earth shall be loosened in heaven." This is the basic premise of faith, and the function of the cerebral computer for our physical body and mortal consciousness. According to the faith we have, that which we bind in a physical way (Earth) concerns the form and the conditions of our light-body expression (heaven). Whatever debris, error, temporary condition we, with faith, loosen or transmute in our Earth bodies and situations, such affects our spiritual awareness and light-body expression.

Nonetheless, in the first stages of birthing the light body, Peter/faith is uncertain of the new ideas, thus wafts back and forth many times. We must not be discouraged. Through studying, meditating and applying divine principles we build faith in the new thought patterns necessary for our spiritual birth. No one type of inspirational or divinely guided literature can fulfill everyone's needs. But all studies must be based on truth, and should be proven to be the truth. We must repeat this discipline again and again, until it is so secure in our hearts, minds and activities that nothing can loosen it.

Peter again is our living example of what it takes to express true spiritual faith in the I Am Self. He was a fisherman who cast his net to the right and the left, with no success. In the sea of Divine Mind he allowed himself to be buffeted and disjointed and without plan, being cast here and there by the elements of nature. But because Peter was honest and sincere in his search, Jesus—the representative I Am figure —stabilized his wavering trust by advising him, "Cast your net to the right [the conscious-will aspect and the positive-energy polarity of ideas] and you will catch more fish [divine truths] than your net can hold." Peter, our own faith faculty, does this and the net is filled to the brim, but it does not break.

Faith is anchored in us and we become satisfied that we are following the right master. But we are not expressing yet our faith to the total expectation and needs of our I Am Self. Jesus asked Peter to feed his sheep (the flock or the citizens of the I Am consciousness to be built on the mortal, physical, Earth plane). Three times he asked him to do this, meaning it has to be done on three levels: mental, emotional and astral (soul or past memories and experiences relating to previous incarnations here on Earth or elsewhere in the cosmos). If faith is nurtured on all three of these levels (lower bodies), the physical manifestation is automatic, because the physical is the fourth and final outpicturing of functionings from the first three levels or bodies of our mortal being.

We must transmute all three levels before we can expect the light body to be birthed fully through our physical, Earth form. Remember, when Jesus did resurrect the light form on that first Easter morning, he said to Mary in the garden at the tomb, "Do not touch me, for I have not yet ascended to my Father." Viewed from our present-day understanding of the transmutation of the physical form into the light-body frequency, Jesus meant that he had not aligned, adjusted or synchronized all the levels of consciousness (the four lower bodies) to the light-body manifestation. In fact, initially Mary did not recognize the man in the garden as the master Jesus, for she addressed him, "Gardener, have you seen the body of my master who was buried in this tomb?" She did not recognize the transformed countenance of Jesus in his light body.

In the drama of Jesus and the Twelve, our Christ pattern maker asked Peter/faith, not once but three times, "Do you love me?" Does your faith love the Christ Self and the process of transmuting the physical, mortal

16

personality into the light-body manifestation on all three levels: mental, emotional and soul?

We will have to work with each of the three levels separately and in conjunction with each other before we can effect perfect alignment, and thus birth the light body through our present physical form. Using the appropriate color technique on each of the three levels will aid in transmuting and firmly planting that characteristic for that area. Our work will not be completed by just one or two sessions, but will require many efforts throughout our life development.

Most of what manifests in our physical bodies, experiences and relationships is a direct result or outpicturing of mental, emotional and astral episodes of this lifetime and past lives. Until we transmute and align our four lower bodies—and thus manifest the perfect faith of our I Am Self—the higher frequency of the immortal, fourth dimensional, light body cannot supersede the mortal, third dimensional, physical body.

Again, in the initial stages our degree of faith fluctuates; we are unsteady. Peter portrays the dramatic example when he tentatively walks on the water toward Jesus. Faith steps out on uncharted waters (new spiritual ideas); yet falters, even sinks. But if the seeker (Peter) is determined and steady (aligned with or joined in his search with his brother Andrew, who represents the second divine characteristic of strength–stability–steadfastness), then he finds greater resolve. He calls out to the Master (Christ consciousness) to save him. Buoyed by the confidence and faith of the immortal Self, he is lifted above the unsteady waves of his mortal fears and emotions.

In limitations or diseases of the physical body, such unsteadiness is clearly apparent. Unreliable faith will cause mental anguish; express disbelief in healing possibilities; use rational, physically based arguments against the newfound metaphysical, spiritual approaches to healing; and thereby lead to various cerebral diseases such as headaches. Denial—as Peter proved three times during Jesus' trial—is the classic reaction to any diagnosis of disease, disharmony and dysfunction in our lives. Peter, which is faith, must think, must know, must *be* before he has pledged his full allegiance to the Christ Self.

As we establish our church, or build the I Am Self acceptance into the mind/cerebrum, the light body can start to anchor into the physical, third dimension. But if faith in the freshly developing Self wavers, the foundation (the cerebral receiving-and-sending centers) will start to crumble and the whole building process could fall.

Jesus, showing us the Christ way, cemented the rock-solid cornerstone of divine faith. Commending his spirit to the Father (I Am), he demonstrated total, unwavering faith in his God Self when he was crucified and entombed. Via faith and the reprograming of the cerebrum, the central computer, after three days the Master resurrected his light body on Earth.

PHYSICAL DATA
Cerebrum of Brain

The cerebrum is the largest and uppermost section of the brain, which is housed within the protective confines of the skull. (See Figure 1.) The cerebrum contains an estimated seventy-five billion neurons or nerve cells. These cells and their interconnecting nerve fibers form the structural components of this marvelous computer, which is smaller yet more complex and efficient than any computer presently known to man.

The cerebrum consists of two cerebral hemispheres. In general, the left cerebral hemisphere controls the activities of the right side of the body, whereas the right cerebral hemisphere controls the activities of the left side of the body. The left cerebral hemisphere also is the principal physical site for conscious mind functions such as analysis, logic and decision-making. Subconscious mind functions such as intuition, symbolic thinking and image formation are programed primarily in and through the right cerebral hemisphere. Within both hemispheres, numerous centers exist where specific functions occur, such as hearing, vision, touch, speech and muscular control.

Imbalances or blockages in the faith characteristic at mental, emotional and astral-soul levels may cause bioelectrical, biochemical or structural disturbances in the cerebrum. However, these abnormal changes may not be sufficient to cause discernible symptoms or specific diseases. Instead, the difficulties in faith may manifest primarily in one's words or deeds.

On other occasions, problems with faith may cause cerebral imbalances that produce headaches. The cerebrum itself does not have pain receptors, so it does not experience pain. However, the coverings of the cerebrum (the meninges), the muscles on the scalp and the blood vessels in the head do have sensory nerves that record pain. The two most common types of headaches are tension and migraine headaches. Tension headaches are caused by painful contraction of muscles around the scalp

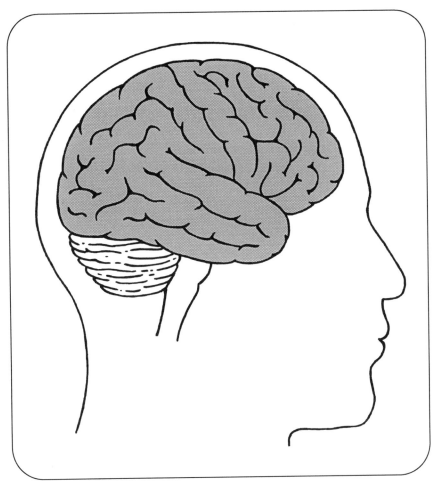

Figure 1. Lateral view of cerebrum (shaded).

and the neck. Migraines stem from the painful dilation of blood vessels in the head; and may be accompanied by visual disturbances, nausea and vomiting, and sensitivity to light and sound.

Extensive self-analysis of the faith characteristic is not required each time a headache occurs. The headache may be simply the result of a stressful day, or it may have a physical cause such as noxious fumes, chemicals in foods, reactions to medications or weather changes. Moreover, a neck massage, a short nap or meditation, or taking an analgesic may remove the pain, without recurrence.

Headaches also may stem from disorders in other parts of the body, such as high blood pressure, constipation, eye strain or sinusitis. Therefore, in both diagnosis and treatment, one must consider the whole body and not just its separate parts.

If head pain is intense or accompanied by fever, mental disturbances or loss of consciousness, consult a physician immediately. For treatment, follow a holistic approach, using the best of all effective remedies.

When headaches have no physical cause, occur frequently and are not relieved by common treatments, it is essential to focus on the faith characteristic. Examine how doubts, fears of failure, insecurities, lack of confidence, or other blockages in faith may be the cause of your headaches. Reprogram these imbalances by fortifying your faith in your I Am Self and in divine truths, by manifesting the faith *of* your high Self. Your headaches will be healed.

Blockages in faith also may be the primary or a contributing cause of more serious cerebral disorders, such as epilepsy and benign and malignant brain tumors. These diseases always require prompt medical attention and treatment, including appropriate medication and surgery. But if full healing is to occur, attention also must be given to the spiritual quality of faith, since it directly and specifically influences the health of the cerebrum.

No matter how minor or major the cerebral illness, regardless of its cause (physical, genetic, psychological, or soul imbalances carried over from past lives), via faith in one's inherent wholeness and holiness as a child of God, the cerebrum is healed.

COLOR VISUALIZATION
Royal Blue

Visualize an inverted pyramid of pure white light, starting two or three feet above the physical head. The point of this pyramid penetrates into the cerebrum of the brain. This represents the light-body form of your I Am Self entering into your crown chakra/cerebrum.

Think about having the faith *of* God inserted through this exercise. The white light slowly becomes blue light, even a blue liquid pouring down into the cerebrum. Gradually turning royal blue, the fluid light bathes and submerges the entire brain. Through the brain, this royal-blue substance travels to every part of the body. As it does, the faith *of* God pours into every pore and cell of the physical, making you, a child of God, one with the Father-Mother Creator.

Because it is so important that faith and love be combined for the proper and lasting demonstration, visualize the liquid blue substance flowing from the brain directly to the heart. When faith *of* God and love of God become equally strong in the consciousness, we can say to any part of our bodies: be healed, be changed, be in another place, perform this function. Faith in the law of God and love of God's law demand immediate obedience and eventual results.

Finally, to complete this exercise, visualize the liquid blue light spilling down from the crown center/cerebrum like a waterfall, splashing over the entire auric field that extends one-to-two feet from the physical body. The aura is composed of the astral, the emotional and the mental bodies. Each of these three bodies has to receive the healing blue waters of faith in God and the faith *of* God; which we, as His-Her children, must express if we are to demonstrate the light body of our I Am Self. From these levels faith will penetrate into our physical form. The physical will permit birth of the light form only according to the faith anchored into the auric field.

As each of the three levels of the auric field incorporates the light frequency of each of the twelve divine characteristics, such as faith in this case, physical transmutation will begin. We must expect and accept this. Transmutation occurs because in these three levels there still are blockages which prohibit the full implantation of the higher aspect of that characteristic. Hence, blockages in faith prevent the proper flow of energy into the crown chakra and cerebrum, resulting in malfunction of the central computer. However, by removing the blockage and by implanting a higher level of faith in the cerebrum, we heal the cerebral dysfunction.

SONG INSPIRATION
Faith

Where are the keys to the kingdom?
Where lies the golden crown?
Where is this rock I'm to build upon?
Where is faith to be found?
What can I believe in?
What can I believe in?
Where is faith to be found?

21

Fears and worries try to catch me in the dark:
Am I going to die,
Or lose what I'm holding tightly to?
I cry out, I'm so afraid!
What can I believe in?
What can I believe in?
Where is faith to be found?

Then walking toward me on the water
I saw myself as I Am,
With keys of truth and the golden crown.
I see I had them all along.
Now I know what to believe in!
Now I know what to believe in!
I know where faith is found.

Faith is where I always put it.
Wherever I put it, it was strong.
It was strong in fear, but now it's clear
It can be strong in the light.
This I can believe in!
This I can believe in!
You know that it feels so right.

I put my faith in God's order.
I put my faith in His love.
I put my faith in unchanging law.
I put my faith in I Am.
This I can believe in!
This I can believe in!
This is the faith I have found.

2. Strength

Metaphysical Interpretation: *Andrew*

Physical Data: *Spinal Cord & Nerves*

Color Visualization: *Lemon Yellow*

Song Inspiration: *Strength*

METAPHYSICAL INTERPRETATION
Andrew

The apostle Andrew was Peter's brother and partner in the fishing business, and immediately joined Jesus the Christ following his brother's conversion. Peter accepted that the Messiah had come to Israel. Israel is the congregation of our spiritual thoughts; one body, one nation. Strength is the second necessary characteristic we consciously must build for manifestation of the light body.

Strength–stability–steadfastness externalizes as the spinal cord and the nerves, which function as a communications system for the cerebrum computer to send information, computations and decisions to, and to receive information from, the rest of the body parts.

Faith/cerebrum and strength/spinal cord and nerves are positive-active and negative-receptive polarities (action-reaction) of the first divine principle; they form the first of the six pairs of basic attributes of our Father-Mother God. This initial pair, strength equal with faith, is part of the trinity of the Son of God involuting into matter. Peter and Andrew were the sons of John, whose name spiritually means *love*. Faith and strength, therefore, are the products of divine love.

Contemplate the dictionary definitions for each one of these Andrew qualities. *Strength*: endurance, power, stamina. *Stability*: permanence, durability, calmness, resistance to chemical or physical change. *Steadfastness*: determination, loyalty, faithfulness, reliability, unchangeability, firmness.

At lesser degrees of spiritual unfoldment, we have to deal with crystallized realizations and patterns of our mortal concepts. But in later stages, when we fully birth the light body, we must anticipate and work consciously with new approaches, ideas and applications. At the lesser steps, we undoubtedly demonstrate a modicum of patience, some ability to survive obstacles and oppositions to goals, perseverance in spiritual studies. More than likely, at this degree in the anchoring of the light form, we are teachers of these same lessons for other students. In fact, often we must demonstrate endurance through many hardships, and likely must survive competition and opposition from those who are expressing similar interests but who have not the highest expressions of divine love in action.

But all of these challenges still are not full spiritual strength, nor are they the power and the stamina required to *complete* the birth of the light body. True, they may be cousins and friends in the light, but they are not blood brothers of faith.

When we give undivided and undiluted attention to the strength characteristic, automatically there will be a stress on the spinal cord and the nerves. This stress may manifest as pain and discomfort in the neck and arms; as irritation in the low back and down the sciatic nerve to the legs; or as malfunctioning of the internal organs, whose functions are regulated by nerve impulses. Irritability, edginess and nervousness also may accompany pain and inflammation.

Therefore, as indicated already, in analyzing physical-body conditions metaphysically, we must begin to correlate any difficulties, diseases, lack of harmony in the spinal cord and the nerves with corresponding attitudes and spiritual applications concerning the concepts of strength, determination, stability of and steadfastness to the I Am Self.

To avoid overzealousness in correlating physical-body systems with the divine characteristics of the I Am Self, we should understand that every system of the physical vehicle is linked with the cerebrum by way of the nerves. Therefore, it may take professional medical diagnosis to determine whether the originating cause of the physical problem stems from actual impairment of the body part experiencing the disharmony or disease, or from dysfunction of the nerves that carry bioelectrical impulses from the cerebrum to that body part.

Additionally, we must examine strength–stability–steadfastness (1) in the mental and intellectual aspects of our individual self, (2) in the emotional and feeling nature, and (3) in the astral-memory aspects of this lifetime and past incarnations. All three aspects contribute to the physical stamina and strength developing for the full birth of the light body of our I Am Self.

Thus, it becomes necessary to review and to develop those conditions where mental steadfastness, strength and endurance are required. Sometimes several lifetimes are needed before we can remain steadfast to the determination and the intention of following the cosmic laws of life.

On an emotional level, patience and perseverance are commendable. But all of us have experienced varying types of depression, fear of being wrong, hurt from being misunderstood. Before our light body can be reborn, we must deal with all these emotions and totally eliminate them.

To look at the attribute of strength strictly from the physical aspect essentially is to miss the point. Consider this: there have been athletes and warriors beyond number on this Earth planet who generally have proven little, as far as spiritual strength and stability are concerned. They might be admired, even emulated, for their perseverance and demonstrations on the physical. But unless their mental, emotional and character-building aspects of life are in equal proportion to these physical attributes, their physical prowess contributes little to the spiritual birth of the I Am.

However, with this important exception and also with the intention of not downgrading the importance of physical health and strength, unless the physical body and all of its systems are in excellent balance and harmony, they cannot sustain the tremendous stress of spiritual energies and the necessary physical transmutation process. Our cells quite literally may experience agonizing changes as the light body anchors in and through the physical body. Therefore, it is vital that the physical body be able to withstand the serious and difficult experiences which transmutation causes.

Such strength in the physical body relies predominantly on the spinal cord and the nerves. For whenever there is a lessening of Andrew/strength in our mind or emotions, an immediate problem may arise in this system. Mental, emotional and psychic-astral conditions instantly reflect into the physical body and cause some degree of nerve dysfunction. Our communicational nervous system responds immediately to the slightest doubt or lack of steady application to the goal of becoming the I Am incarnate on the physical dimension.

Obviously, the strength must come from an equal degree of faith. No matter what happens around the spiritually determined individual, no matter how difficult the task appears to be, no matter how many problems are involved in performing the task or the mission delegated, that steadiness and strength (which are manifested through the physical form via the nerves) must be able to carry the impulses and the messages to the various parts of our body, which is our personal I Am nation we are building on Earth. Each of those cells/citizens must be able to depend permanently on Andrew/strength/spinal cord and nerves.

Any deviation of that strength and steadfastness causes an immediate malfunction of the system. The slightest malfunctioning changes the performance of the spiritual mission; and temporarily, even permanently, can disrupt the flow for that time, in that place, for that purpose of that particular life episode.

At this point, we can consider Proverbs 18:10–11: "The name of the

Lord is a tower of strength, where the righteous may run for refuge. A rich man's wealth is his strong city, a towering wall, so he supposes." The *name* of the Lord is the *nature* of the Lord. The *Lord* symbolizes the *laws of God*. That nature is strength and is a refuge for all. The *tower* is our spine; the hidden wealth of a strong city or personal nation is the I Am Self.

Again, because of the nature of the nerves, we have to emphasize purity, cleanliness, purification of mind and body and soul. During rebalancing and transmutation, a great deal of debris from the mind, the soul and the emotions is poured into all of the body's systems, affecting directly and immediately the physical expression. This outpouring of our memories, regrets, new resolutions and higher insights causes a corresponding change in our body cells. Some cells die; some are transformed. All of them must be refined and purified so that they can anchor the higher frequencies of the light body.

Strength and determination are threatened by this cleansing or transmutation. Unless there is no flagging in our spiritual determination to eliminate all our old patterns and our conscious acceptance of less-than-perfect mortal demonstrations, the physical toxins and debris will become so great that physical disease and impairment are inevitable.

So, at each new step in birthing the light body, we may be required to give up even more of the various unhealthy physical foods and to concentrate more than ever on the higher frequency forms such as fruits and vegetables. During all light-body experiences, we must keep our physical form in a steady balance through sufficient supply of protein, vitamins, minerals and other essential nutrients.

PHYSICAL DATA
Spinal Cord & Nerves

Like the cerebrum, the spinal cord and the nerves are composed of neurons or nerve cells that transmit bioelectrical impulses. The spinal cord exits from the base of the skull and continues to the lower part of the back. (See Figure 2.) Spinal vertebrae that make up the backbone, which also is called the vertebral or spinal column, surround the delicate spinal cord and protect it from injury.

Nerve tracts in the spinal cord carry impulses or messages from the brain, down the spinal cord, and out through thirty-one pairs of spinal nerves to muscles, glands and other organs. The spinal nerves also carry

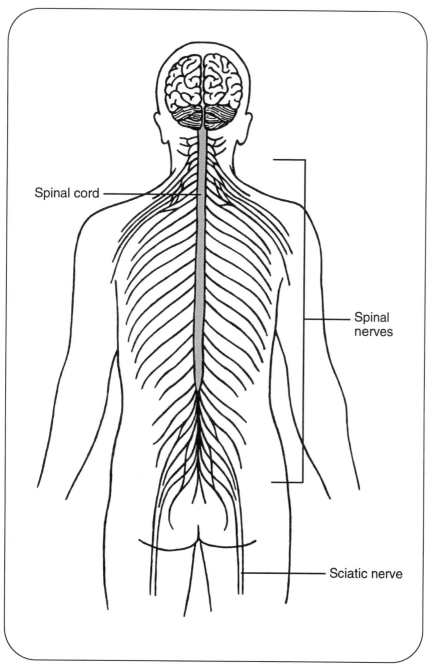

Figure 2. Spinal cord and nerves.

sensory nerve impulses from numerous parts of the body to the spinal cord, wherein they ascend to the brain.

Twelve pairs of cranial nerves pass through other openings in the skull. They transmit impulses from the brain to organs in the head, neck, chest and abdomen; and from these areas to the cerebrum.

There are three major types of nerves. Sensory nerves carry information from sensory organs—such as the eyes, the ears and the touch receptors—to the cerebral computer. Motor nerves transmit impulses from the cerebrum to muscles that are required for movement. Autonomic nerves, both sympathetic and parasympathetic divisions, carry messages to organs that usually are not under our conscious control.

From a spiritual standpoint, the spine serves as a conduit or a channel for the flow of energy. In Eastern symbology, the kundalini is depicted as rising up the spine when we refine and uplift our thoughts, feelings, memories and physical form. In the Star of David, this is represented by the upward-pointing triangle. In the birth of the light body, however, the fiery light of the I Am Self flows down the spine. The primary contact point with the light body is the crown chakra/cerebrum. From there, the spine transfers the higher light frequencies down to the other chakras and along the nerves to all physical organs. In the Star of David, this is symbolized by the downward-pointing triangle.

Mental, emotional and soul-astral imbalances in the strength characteristic may be the primary or a contributing cause of neuritis or nerve inflammation. This may manifest as pain, tingling or numbness in the back of the neck, in the shoulders and arms, along the spinal cord, in the low back, or along the sciatic nerve in the leg. Difficulties with strength also may cause nerve disorders such as multiple sclerosis, Bell's palsy, trigeminal neuralgia, Guillain-Barré syndrome, and shingles.

To correct any nerve disorder, follow a holistic approach that centers around the spiritual quality of strength–stability–steadfastness. Refine and reinforce this divine attribute via affirmation, decree, visualization and realization. Be a tower of strength.

If symptoms persist or are severe, see a physician. Take whatever medication, vitamin or herbal remedy, or undergo any treatment, which has been proven to be therapeutic. Meditation, counseling, dream interpretation, or a soul reading by a competent psychic may reveal the underlying psychological or past-life causes of the nerve imbalance.

With spinal or back pain, in addition to neuritis consider numerous other possible physical causes. Muscle and ligament strains, muscle spasms, poor posture, trauma to the spine, arthritis, misalignment of the vertebrae, or spinal tumors may cause back pain. A slipped or prolapsed disc in the low back may press on the sciatic nerve and cause sciatica.

Spinal manipulation as performed by chiropractors, some osteopaths and a few medical doctors may relieve back pain and may help to restore nerve function by adjusting and realigning the spinal vertebrae. Massage, acupuncture, pressure-point therapies, B vitamin supplementation, and exercise also may be key components of a comprehensive treatment program.

From the mortal level we cannot dictate the time or the way in which Spirit heals our spinal cord and nerves. Sometimes our decrees and visualizations manifest quickly, so that other therapies are not required. Or we may spend weeks, months, years or a lifetime reviewing, reevaluating and reprograming the soul errors that are the principal causes of our nerve dysfunction. Physically, we may prefer to rely primarily on nutritional supplements or hands-on therapies, only to discover that medication or surgery is the best treatment for our condition. If we steadfastly persevere in our holistic healing efforts, however, the strength and stability we envision eventually will manifest in our spinal cord and nerves. What we see, will be.

COLOR VISUALIZATION
Lemon Yellow

When the spinal cord and the nerves are agitated or inflamed, visualize yellow in its full potential. Breathe it in as sunlight. See it healing, warming, strengthening all resolve and stabilizing all weaknesses. Wear or carry something bright yellow.

How do you know when to stop using the bright yellow? In meditation, ask your I Am Self for guidelines. As the need for the sun-yellow strength and steadfastness fades for that series of implantations (and remember, there are many repeated cycles for the implanting of each characteristic), there will be a diminishing of the lemon-yellow shade during sincere endeavors to hold on to that particular visualization. Gradually the color will fade until it becomes a whitish yellow. White is the next color in the progressive order of spiritual characteristics to be implanted for I Am manifestation. Asking for guidance, accept it as you receive it. Trust your I Am Self to be in control of the birth of your light body.

SONG INSPIRATION
Strength

Beyond the scope of what we see
Are plans to map the future;
And if we allow, our parts will fit the whole.
Behind the scenes the masters work with all the many
  pieces.
Before the hour strikes again, our turn to serve may come.

chorus
Strength, stability, ah, steadfastness.
Strength, stability, stand fast, don't lose control.

Beside us as we go ahead
Are those who love and guide us.
They are there when we cry out, and we shall never fall.
Before us is a magnificent dream;
We are the backbone of a brand-new nation.
As we move on, as we stand strong, the Earth is born again.

chorus
Strength, stability, ah, steadfastness.
Strength, stability, stand fast, don't lose control.

Between us there is much love.
We've been here together;
Many lives, many loves, memories to treasure.
Because our strength is found in love
Our future is much brighter.
As we move on, our love is strong, and we are born again.

chorus
Strength, stability, ah, steadfastness.
Strength, stability, stand fast, don't lose control.

3. Love

Metaphysical Interpretation: *John*

Physical Data: *Heart & Circulatory System*

Color Visualization: *White*

Song Inspiration: *Love*

METAPHYSICAL INTERPRETATION
John

Love is the mantle of protection, from first to last, in the birth of the light body. Each of the twelve divine characteristics which support the I Am Self in its activities has been dramatized through the life of Jesus. Love, being of supreme importance, is no exception.

When Jesus' mother, Mary, became pregnant, she visited her cousin Elizabeth, who likewise was with child. The Gospel of Luke informs us that Elizabeth's child—later to become the one to herald the Messiah's arrival—"leaped for joy in her womb." This was John, literally meaning *love*. It is love that recognizes the potential of the unborn Christ consciousness. It becomes a voice in the wilderness of our mortal, earthly ways and conditions, crying out to us: repent; be humble; prepare, cleanse and purify your mind, body and soul, for I Am coming.

This same John or love characteristic in us prepares the others who will serve the I Am Self. Simon Peter/faith; his brother Andrew/strength; the two sons of Zebedee, John/love and James/wisdom, were disciples of John the Baptist. These four basic attributes, which are needed to build the whole body of the I Am Self, already had been cleansed and prepared by the first awakening of mortal love for the immortal or divine love, before Jesus was ready to call them unto him.

The four disciples had consulted initially with the prophet John, who was their first teacher. He told them: "Follow him. He is the one for whom I have been preparing you. I am not even worthy to unlatch his shoelaces."

Throughout Jesus' ministry, it is said his favorite disciple was John, referred to as the Beloved. At Jesus' final hour, again it is John/divine love who is at the foot of the cross. He is the only disciple during the crucifixion–resurrection initiation to remain steadfast and selfless. It is John to whom Christ Jesus gives final instructions. It is John/divine love to whom the I Am entrusts its soul/Mary the Mother when the physical form must release to death, to await transmutation in and resurrection from the tomb.

Therefore, it is the love characteristic which recognizes the signs impregnated in our being signifying that the I Am is ready for birth. It must be dependable and faithful throughout all trials and temptations. It serves unfailingly during our transmutation, which takes us from the initial anchoring of the light body in the physical form to the actual birth or resurrection of the light body.

Love is the most talked about, most needed, most sought after, most misused of all spiritual characteristics. Divine love, to which we are referring, is not concerned with personality traits and individual characteristics. But humankind in general, because of its limited viewpoint and understanding, has come to worship personality traits, not spiritual qualities. The love which the I Am projects is that same quality which Spirit expresses by creating an infinite variety of species and individualities.

The I Am Self is that part of humanity which is eternal, impersonal, creative and indestructible. It is that part of us that emulates our Father-Mother God and His-Her divine love attributes. Therefore, in I Am consciousness each individual loves all of Spirit's creations. But in human consciousness we have misused Spirit's creations, including our own I Am image. In our confusion and error conditions, as a result of the fall into matter and the subsequent loss of spiritual memory, we have lost our original perspective and our relationships with all other created forms. It has taken us eons and repeated incarnations to remember that all creation originates from the one and the same Source: Spirit, the Creator.

During our evolution back to this original state of I Am, we reexperience what Jesus did when he instructed all of us, as his disciples, to love our enemies. In our reinstatement to Christhood, we realize there are no enemies, whether persons or conditions, against which we have to fight. For truly in this state we love them all in the divine sense, regardless of their errors. "Father, forgive them, for they know not what they do."

The pain we feel for those who lie, who slander us, who deliberately distort, who hurt and misunderstand us, who try to destroy us or our works becomes as a sword piercing the heart. This is the crucifixion. When our motives are pure and the love of God for each of His-Her creations and individualized expressions is active in our consciousness, the crucifixion we suffer mentally, emotionally and karmically is beyond any physical torture or time element. It can last for hours, days, years, lifetimes until the resurrection brings forth our light body.

Jesus never said, "*I* forgive those who harm me and demand my crucifixion." He, of his individualized personality self, could not forgive them. But the Father, the I Am Self within, does forgive. Only from that level can the forgiveness and the absolution from the sin or the error have any worthwhile effect. Lip service on the physical or intellectual levels, or even an emotional forgiveness, is not enough. It has no lasting or permanent effect. Only the I Am part of ourselves, the Father within, can forgive destructive forces.

Until we reach the level Jesus demonstrated in his three years of ministry, it really is most difficult to express sincerely divine love and forgiveness for those who attempt to destroy honest and true spiritual works, thoughts and feelings.

Consider this: denying the *good* in another actually is denying the *God* in another. Since we all are created from this one God Source, specifically and directly it signifies the person is attempting to deny his own God Source. Jesus faced this situation many times; as he did also in other lifetimes, such as when he incarnated as Moses and Socrates.

Therefore, only when we establish a real connection from the Source of our own I Am Self to that of another can we really reverse the trend and decrystallize such thought patterns. When that love and forgiveness come from the I Am, we dissolve the outer actions and can redirect the energies of spiritual love.

It is through the trinity principle of our Father-Mother God, manifesting as the Son (divine love), that all individualizations are created, be they personality beings, species, races, dimensions, planets and so forth. Our Parent God knows the self-will of His-Her creation of mankind, the Son of God. It was freely given. As children made in the image and likeness of our Creator, we must learn how to use divine power, will, faith. But we must use them with divine love. "He who knows the Father, recognizes me, the son. He who recognizes me as the son, sees the Father in me."

This divine principle explains why the personality or individualized mortal self cannot forgive error against the Christ Self and its works. Only the I Am, which had directed those experiences into the life, can forgive with love (give love for) all the pain, fear, hatred, even death caused by others.

The I Am loves whatever situation or condition occurs in the environment, to the society, within the family, or with our personal affairs. It has directed these to us for the spiritual crossing-out-and-over to the I Am consciousness and light-body experience. Every situation therefore becomes a golden opportunity, a series of individual scenes within an eternal cosmic drama, for the mortal, personality self to unify with the immortal, I Am Self—thereby bringing the light body into full birth.

Jesus, hearing the very persons whom he had healed and helped, demand, "Crucify him!" did not descend into mortal reactions of resentment, disgust, anger and retaliation. Even in the face of physical death he knew, by the spiritual love within him, that he was the mirror of their consciences. By his actions and teachings he knew he had demonstrated to those citizens of Israel (the congregation of spiritual thoughts) how far from the mark of a truly spiritual life they had fallen.

In our own cosmic drama, even those spiritual ideas, not regenerated at this point of our development, want to remove from our midst any reminder that we are not living what we believe and teach; that we are hypocrites to ourselves and our associates. Jesus, then as now, is the personification of this ultimate degree of I Am Self expression. In essence, our citizens/thoughts/cells cry out to destroy the spiritual Self when divine love demands too much of our mortal status quo and comfort.

But never can we destroy the immortal part of ourselves. We only can postpone the inevitable work of preparing ourselves to live it, to be it. The immortal I Am rises up amongst our mortal attitudes and actions again and again and again.

In its confusion and error the mortal self wants to believe the immortal I Am is in error, is to blame for sufferings and discomfort, desires to remove the freewill gift of individual choice. From its limited view and understanding of earthly conditions—be they environmental problems, sociological or governmental or family situations, health, finances and so forth—the mortal self belittles, undermines, attempts to destroy whatever the I Am Self has brought into the light of consciousness for examination and judgment.

Spiritual teachers and leaders through the ages have been aware of this technique mortal man uses: God or His agents, such as prophets and way showers, are to blame for all the troubles on Earth. But the I Am Self, this spark in us which is the child of our Parent Creator, knows better and continues to love, to direct, to inspire, to create new and varied conditions in order to awaken the mortal self to those attributes of the immortal Self.

In the overall evolvement of humankind, those new and varied conditions can involve a particular hierarchal plan developed specifically by those who have reached the I Am state of consciousness. The plan may take thousands of years, creating specific conditions and environments and societies for the group of souls who need to experience them. Such a plan is in operation today: the Latter Days, the War of Armageddon, the

Mark Age period and program, the end of this level of consciousness; which, in effect, is the end of this mortal world as we now know it.

The immortal, I Am Self directs those life experiences to the mortal, personality self from which the individual can learn and grow through certain relationships; circumstances of birth, society and environment; occupational opportunities; economic situations; health conditions, and so forth. This is the way karma, both good and bad, is balanced. Therefore, our I Am Self permits whatever is occurring for the benefit of our mortal counterpart or personality creation. But our mortal self, due to its limited nature, cannot see the I Am Self's motives. The mortal self's reactions—be they anger, resentment, hatred, destruction, blame or whatever—do not influence or change the purposes, the intentions, the plans of our I Am Self.

Because of this almost automatic reflex reaction from our mortal level, regarding our I Am Self decisions and actions, it is rather obvious why we must implant the characteristic of strength–stability–steadfastness early in the birth of our light body. The challenges and the pain to the system brought about by love, which requires change and transmutation and repentance, necessitate the strength and the stability of the Andrew aspect. As the heart center becomes activated and the love/ circulatory system begins to transmute the impurities from experiences and thoughts, the spinal cord and the nerves had better be in a healthy, balanced condition in order to withstand this cleansing which God's love for us produces.

But it is important to heed this warning: In spite of the fact that we work at accepting and implanting these spiritual qualities in ourselves *many times*, the birthing of the light body is not complete with one or two or a thousand experiences, meditations and determinations. For some, depending on how much karma and soul cleansing are involved, it may take several lifetimes to achieve the full birth. Do not become discouraged or weary.

That is why the implanting of each of these spiritual characteristics follows a divine pattern, a specific sequence. The first two apostles/ characteristics must be called into action first. Peter is the rock of faith, the first active principle or character in this drama of Christ birth in ourselves. Faith correlates with the cerebrum, which serves as the primary contact point with the light body and as a central computer station for our thoughts, feelings, memories and actions. Then Andrew, the receptive half of this brother partnership, brings strength–stability–steadfastness to the cause. The spinal cord and the nerves are a communications system which serves the cerebrum and our faith in carrying out our responsibilities.

When the apostle John characteristic, the next positive-active principle in this dramatization, establishes every relationship, experience and circumstance—which must be lived through; must be conquered with and ordained for love divine—then the body, the mind and the soul can withstand all reactions resulting from every experience and relationship.

Jesus demonstrated this divine love again in the Garden of Gethsemane. Tired, hurt, confused, betrayed, unsure of even his closest disciples, he prayed that not his mortal will but the Father's will, the will of the I Am within, be done. Facing suffering, even death, love must conquer all things.

PHYSICAL DATA
Heart & Circulatory System

The spiritual quality of love externalizes via the heart chakra as the heart and the circulatory system, which includes the liver, the spleen, the blood vessels, the blood and the lymphatic system. (See Figure 3.)

The heart is a muscular organ that beats rhythmically, pumping blood through arteries to the capillaries. These minute vessels have small openings that allow the blood's contents to diffuse into the fluid bathing the cells of all parts of the body; bringing hormones, nutrients, oxygen and other items carried by the blood. Veins carry blood from the capillaries back to the heart.

The blood consists of two components: cells and fluid (plasma). The cells are divided into three major types: red blood cells, white blood cells, and platelets. Red blood cells contain hemoglobin, which combines with oxygen. White blood cells protect the body from infection. Platelets are part of the blood-clotting system.

The liver is a transmutation factory that carries out hundreds of chemical reactions. For example, digested nutrients travel in the blood from the small intestine to the liver. The liver processes the nutrients; releases proper amounts of amino acids, fats, sugars and vitamins back into the blood; and stores any excess for future needs. The liver also removes toxic items from the blood and converts them into harmless compounds.

The spleen removes old, worn-out red blood cells from the blood,

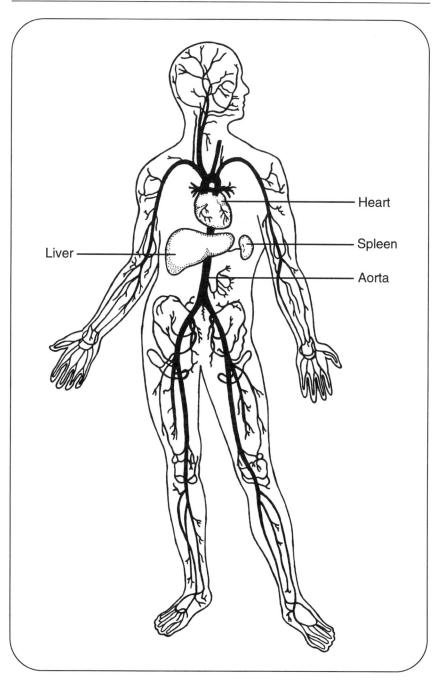

Figure 3. Circulatory system.

retaining the iron from the hemoglobin and storing it for future use. The spleen also removes and destroys microorganisms.

The lymphatic system consists of lymphatic vessels, lymph nodes and the spleen. The lymphatic vessels carry fluid, proteins and other compounds away from the cells back to veins near the heart. The lymph nodes and the spleen produce and contain lymphocytes, a type of white blood cell that is a key component of the immune system. B lymphocytes produce antibodies that attack bacteria and viruses. T lymphocytes destroy parasites, cancer cells, fungi and transplants of foreign tissue.

The interaction of love with the heart and the circulatory system is perhaps the most commonly accepted direct correlation between one of the twelve spiritual characteristics and its corresponding physical system. This can be seen in speech patterns that describe our feelings. We speak of love welling up in our heart; of opening our heart to others. Those who are unloving are called heartless, coldhearted or cold-blooded. When separated from a loved one, we say our heart aches or is broken. When someone speaks angrily, he may be said to vent his spleen.

Moreover, numerous scientific studies have begun to document the correlation between love and the circulatory system. In the 1950s, Drs. Friedman and Rosenman postulated that individuals with Type A personality—who are hostile, self-involved, impatient and always in a hurry —had significantly more coronary heart disease than those with Type B personality, who lack these traits. (In coronary heart disease, the coronary arteries, which supply blood to heart muscle, may be narrowed or closed off by atherosclerotic plaque.) More recent research has shown that the psychological factors most damaging to the heart include hostility, self-involvement and cynicism.

Love is the mantle of protection. When Harvard students watched a film of Mother Teresa demonstrating selfless love, the immunoglobulin-A content in their saliva increased sharply; this IgA antibody destroys viruses. Conversely, researchers found that patients who scored above the average in loneliness had significantly poorer immune functioning. Another study documented that the more people felt loved and supported, the less coronary heart disease they had.

Excessive fat in the diet, smoking, obesity and lack of exercise increase the risk of developing cardiovascular disease. But whether or not these or other physical factors are present, blockages in the spiritual quality of love may cause circulatory disorders. These include coronary heart disease, heart attack, high blood pressure, congestive heart failure, heart valve disease, irregular heartbeats (arrhythmia), hepatitis, cirrhosis, anemia, cancer of the white blood cells (leukemia), cancer of the lymph glands (lymphoma), AIDS (wherein a virus destroys T cell lympho-cytes), and autoimmune disorders (wherein the body makes antibodies against its own cells).

Love is the key in healing all disease, especially heart and circulatory disorders. Studies have proven that a holistic program which includes a low-fat diet, exercise and counseling to remove love blockages reverses coronary heart disease. Opening the heart to let Christ love flow through opens narrowed coronary arteries. Love and forgiveness also stimulate the immune system, which protects all parts of the body from disease caused by infectious agents and keeps the physical form free of tumors. Loving God and loving one another heal mind, body and soul.

COLOR VISUALIZATION
White

In implanting divine love through the heart and the circulatory sys-tem, visualize white light coming down through the crown center, filling the brain, then entering the bloodstream. This brings purity into that system which feeds and nourishes every cell/citizen of the body. See white light purifying, cleansing, transmuting every drop of blood, every vein, every artery in the precious body temple. For this temple will house the nation of thoughts, feelings and experiences that are to bring forth the birth of the light body.

SONG INSPIRATION
Love

With my love I will comfort you
When the trials of life assail you.
With my arms I lovingly embrace you.
I will sustain you.
With my eyes I lovingly behold you.
My heart is a place reserved for all of you.
Can you trust in me just for this moment?
Drinking deeply of my love you will be healed.

43

Then with your love you will bring comfort to the others.
With your arms you'll gently take them in.
With your eyes you will see the light inside them.
For your heart has room for each and every one of them.
And they will trust you just as I trust you;
They'll find comfort in your loving smile.

You will not find in this world a total stranger,
If you only let me in.
Can you trust in me just for this moment?
Drinking deeply of my love you will be healed.
You will not find in this world a total stranger,
If you only let me in,
If you only let me in.

4. Wisdom

Metaphysical Interpretation: *James son of Zebedee*

Physical Data: *Pituitary Gland & Endocrine System*

Color Visualization: *Green*

Song Inspiration: *Wisdom*

METAPHYSICAL INTERPRETATION
James son of Zebedee

Wisdom–justice–judgment is the fourth characteristic to be developed for the resurrection of the mortal form into the immortal, I Am, light body. With this fourth aspect we have the foundation stones to build a solid structure on the third dimensional frequency of Earth, one which can withstand all opposition.

The first of the four basic cosmic building blocks is faith, the rock on which we build our house/light body. The second is strength–stability–steadfastness, the tower or the column of light to hold up our structure. The third is love, the purpose, the ideal, the reason for our nation/temple/body. With these three we have the inverted triangle or trinity anchored into form: faith (Father principle, masculine, positive, activity); strength and stability (Mother principle, feminine, negative, receptivity); and love (Son principle, form, individuality, the child of Father-Mother Creator).

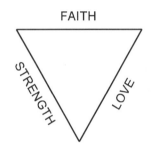

A pertinent channeling from Sananda/Jesus the Christ through me on April 14, 1973, contains these excerpts:

"We wish to create a bar of light across the center of the head—which would symbolically occur—through the ears, across the eyes, in physical relationship. As we do this, we visualize and project another sympathetic energy force of etheric nature [I Am], down through the crown chakra, connecting it with the spine. As you receive these simultaneous energy patterns, you experience the crucifixion initiation. ... It enhances a spiritual connection with the light body or higher Self communion that no other process so far can complete or accelerate. ...

"The dual force relates to the positive and the negative polarities of Creative Energy Itself, the Father-Mother God. With the light body anchoring over the shell of the physical vessel in a pyramidal conclave, you have a trinity force—Father, Mother and Sonship—in equal proportions. ...

"[Man's] Christship with God, the Father-Mother principle, is our essential task in teaching and in demonstrating and in fulfilling, for the minimum of a hundred and forty-four thousand light workers, so that the nucleus is steady and strong and the foundation is of a minimum requirement.*

"You also have been told that the hundred and forty-four thousand represent the cells or the centers within the brain that must be transmuted likewise in you, as it must be transmuted within the race pattern so that the entire race consciousness and the whole form of man in form as a third dimensional being can raise to the fourth dimensional consciousness, and anchor the light-body frequency so that the planet and all life form upon it can be changed likewise and simultaneously. . . .

"Those one hundred and forty-four thousand cellular centers in your brain have to be transformed. . . . Indeed, we contact all your thinking patterns, all your bodily functions and many of your soul blockages through the brain cells or centers, which we just have enumerated in the term of a hundred and forty-four thousand minimum.

"When we wish to transmute a specific central connection with your body, mind or soul, we work solely through the brain apparatus as a central computing station for your three lower aspects of being. After all, you will find, in time, scientifically speaking, all things can be changed, transmuted and controlled via the brain central focus or computing station in the individual man."

From the cosmic trinity we build in the fourth characteristic, the complementary negative-receptive principle of divine wisdom–judgment–justice. The first four apostles were two sets of brothers: Peter/faith and Andrew/strength; and the sons of Zebedee, John/love and James/wisdom. They were called to support the Christ at about the same time and in this particular order. After these four are set in the right direction and for the divine purpose, the I Am Self can build the rest of our body/temple/nation.

In Hebrew, Zebedee literally means *a dowry or a gift of God.* Wisdom and love are graces. John and James' mother, Mary, meaning an aspect of the soul, asked Christ Jesus if her two sons could sit on his right and his left at the coming of his kingdom. Wisdom certainly cannot function without love. Love without wisdom and righteous judgment is a mockery, foolish and silly; sometimes even creating more harm than good.

* The 144,000 elect are the demonstrators and teachers of Christ powers in the Latter Days (1960–2000). The number is literal, in that at least that number must so demonstrate to achieve the spiritual goal of lifting man into the fourth dimension, and symbolic, in that it does not preclude any number of additional ones from being included.

Consider the aspect of wisdom as portrayed in the Old Testament. Solomon was the wisest judge in all of Israel (congregation of spiritual ideas). He was the son of David and Bathsheba. David metaphysically means a form of spiritualized love, a getting ready for the Christ or I Am manifestation. Bathsheba means *seventh daughter*, the soul at the point of spiritual fulfillment. It was Solomon, not David, to whom the Lord, the I Am Self, assigned the building of the Temple of Jerusalem, the nation of peace, our body of light.

Hierarchal channelings through me reveal that King Solomon was an earlier incarnation of Mary, who would be the mother of Jesus. Mary and Jesus are twin souls. The high Self name of Mary is Sol-O-Man, soul of mankind; the matrix or the mother form through which the son becomes manifest. Justice–judgment–wisdom is the architect for building the physical temple or the nation of the I Am. It is out of the house of David that all of Israel waited for its Messiah, the Christ. Solomon was the master builder, mystically and literally. Mary's husband, Joseph, who was a carpenter, was known to have come out of the house of David. Jesus, though immaculately conceived, was the fulfillment of that lineage.

Spiritual wisdom and judgment must come from the soul aspect. For only through the soul memories can we know all the facts of the past, the present and the future, in order to make balanced and righteous judgment of any of the conditions which come up in our lives and consciousnesses for evaluation and final decision. From balancing the scales, weighing all these events and experiences, we can make divine judgments and mete out divine justice.

Justice has been symbolized as a female figure with her eyes blindfolded. She holds up the scales of balance in order to judge properly what is needed further to bring conditions into right order and harmony. The female figure is the negative-receptive polarity of spiritual love, the positive-active polarity. The thoughts, the words and the deeds of humankind are weighed without looking at the outer appearances of things. They are intuitively felt. The all-knowing inner eye, referred to as the third eye in the forehead/pituitary region, weighs and balances, judges and knows what is right. From here the sentence is passed. The reaction, literally and physically, within the body temple is to bring all things in its systems into perfect balance and orderly functioning.

The scales of justice and wisdom are very delicate. They automatically weigh the dotting of every *i*, the crossing of every *t*. Isn't it interesting that even in our written form we have created this symbology as a reminder? The *i* is for the small or mortal "I." The *t* is the crossbar for the mortal, human self crossing over to the immortal, I Am Self.

The scales of justice must be held by the feminine aspect of the soul, because true justice and judgment must come from the full knowledge of each individual's and the group's total karma. Each person affects the group. The group, since it is the sum of all the individuals, affects the development and the opportunities for each individual in it. Therefore, from the cosmic and the hierarchal sense, it takes a master such as Sol-O-Man (Mary, the soul matrix, to form the Christ, I Am body) to help judge the race karma and the individual soul records in our reevolution from the mortal expression into the immortal, light-body form.

The mortal form of justice designed by human cultures never can equate with spiritual or divine justice. For, by its very nature, mortal justice is limited by mortal reasoning. No matter how far back the mortal self goes, it cannot ascertain and place on the scales of balance all that is involved in the mental, the emotional and the soul-psychic regions of individuals or the race.

Spiritual justice (karma) must take into consideration the soul history of the individual as each relates to the entire race history and development. The race history does not involve only all records and civilizations, opportunities and challenges of this particular planet, but also must include the race's experiences and explorations throughout this solar system. For each individual and the race itself have had incarnational experiences throughout many dimensions, planes and planets of this solar system. We have evolved individually—with interrelationships and responsibilities with millions of other souls—and as a group.

Mortal man obviously does not see justice as the immortal Self sees it. Justice by humankind is not tempered by the divine love of Spirit, which measures out Its sentences equally for all parts and individualizations of Its creation.

Was it just for Jesus to suffer as he did? The crucifixion or the death of the physical form was necessary to demonstrate at that point in Earthman's evolutionary progress that there is the resurrection of life, which is the light-body form, a specific individuality expression as a part of the Divine Creator. But what about the sufferings from criticisms, anger, hate, plots and schemes against him by those who actually were the beneficiaries of his teachings and Messiah demonstrations? The greatest to benefit—the priests, scribes, teachers and lawyers of Israel—were the ones who feared him the most and plotted for his assassination. Psychically sensitive, mentally a genius, in cosmic consciousness and feeling, did he not suffer more in those areas than even in the physical crucifixion?

Using both Old and New Testaments for our design and outline of humanity's cosmic drama, to portray in graphic scenes the evolution of the race of man back to its rightful Christ-Son relationship with Father-Mother God, we see now how slowly and perfectly grind the wheels of divine justice. Our pattern maker and way shower is Sananda, who, in Earth incarnations, gave us examples as Moses and Jesus. His soul counterpart, Sol-O-Man, was King Solomon and Mary. Consider the lines of dramatic force developing from Moses, through the house of David, until the final demonstration of the Messiah by Jesus the Christ.

Moses was criticized, hated, plotted against, complained about throughout the forty years of the exodus from Egypt (the subconscious) and the wanderings in the desert. His personal feelings and intellectualizations, his interpretations of divine revelations may not have been as fully developed then as later in his Jesus incarnation. In a sense, as Moses he set up conditions and thought forms which he had to deal with later in the higher, I Am Self consciousness, completed and crossed out as Jesus.

Divine justice, tempered equally with divine love (James and John, gifts of the Lord, I Am), supported and worked with the Christ Self through Jesus of Nazareth to overcome all those thought patterns which had crystallized in Israel and had become a racial pattern, with mortal laws and regulations through the teachings of this same individualization known then as Moses.

The Messiah came to fulfill, not to change, divine revelation and law. By dealing with those same emotions and thoughts which had been channeled to him at a lesser degree of development when he was Moses, over twelve hundred years later he could demonstrate the full initiation and the resurrection, as Jesus. But, cosmically speaking, he did attract—through seemingly slow but methodical divine justice—those situations which needed correction, balance, harmony and just action.

Thus this pattern must be for all the rest of us. In our despair over seemingly unjust accusations, thoughts, words and actions against our higher principles and deeds must come the divine realization that these things are drawn into our orbit, via the simple course of divine wisdom and justice, for spiritual balancing and spiritual judgment. All things

51

presented to us must go through a weighing, a decisive judging process: proper or improper; good for us or serving us ill; constructive or destructive in the building of the spiritual temple, the I Am light-body structure.

Rather than wishing certain conditions and experiences away, rather than retaliating with mortal thinking and rationalizations, we must call for the divine wisdom of the I Am Self to show us the cosmic reasons—past, present and future—why those situations, conditions and relationships are in our path.

Sananda demonstrated both these levels of consciousness for us. As Moses, the son of man, he set forth laws and regulations to aid the mortal body and mind in coming through the slavery of our subconscious (Egypt). As Jesus he had to reap some of the reactions from the Mosaic system and the misuses of the intellectual aspects of the mortal man (scribes and lawyers of the nation). And he taught us in that incarnation how the son of God deals wisely and well, but most firmly, with such abuses of divine law.

In the metaphysical or spiritual sense, divine justice wisely judges and balances the scales of karma. Then immortal, I Am wisdom sentences the mortal self to set into motion all corrections to bring about perfect harmony, just as water seeks its own level.

Whatever occurs in our body/temple/nation is for us to deal with, to know about, and to judge righteously. Weigh all past experiences from the soul memory bank with the future directions and plans for yourself and the race. Take into consideration all surrounding circumstances and visualize the future results of every action, thought and word. Whatever does not serve the future goals of I Am consciousness and expression, eliminate ruthlessly but lovingly. This takes divine wisdom, which is a gift or a dowry from God.

Know, with the surety of the all-knowing and all-seeing eye of the I Am Self within, that everything that is thought about or spoken of goes into the auric field, becoming a thought pattern waiting for physical manifestation. If we do not feed the aura with mental and emotional energy, those thought patterns cannot be born into our experiences. So, judge each thought, word and deed wisely and with spiritual discernment.

In the physical body, over which we must have full mastery and control in order to bring forth the I Am light form, the pituitary gland is the master endocrine gland for controlling the body's functioning. For example, it secretes growth hormone, which regulates the rate of growth of the body. It also controls the water level in the body. Since our physical bodies are comprised of about sixty percent water—just as the planet itself is about one-fourth land mass and three-fourths water—water is the most important constituent of our bodies, in the way that water is the predominant consideration for our lives on this planet.

This master gland sends out hormones in accordance with or equal to the needs of all the other glands of the endocrine system. In addition, the endocrine glands relate physically to the spiritual centers or chakras. For perfect health, balance, harmony and functioning, the pituitary must have a perfect relationship with all the other endocrine glands. It is the master builder. The pituitary, located in the center of the head, is the seat of all-knowingness, the all-seeing eye, the master builder of the light body; just as Solomon was the master builder of the Temple of Jerusalem.

It follows in natural sequential order that since the pituitary is the master endocrine gland and represents our soul aspect through the third-eye region, it is the pivotal point for birthing our light body through our physical form.

Any imperfections in spiritual judgment, any unwise thought patterns, any disregard for endocrine imbalances in our physical body relate to the apostle James, the I Am characteristic of divine wisdom–justice–judgment. Wisdom with love, faith with strength: these four are the first building blocks for the I Am light-body birthing.

PHYSICAL DATA
Pituitary Gland & Endocrine System

There are seven spiritual centers in the light body, seven corresponding chakras or power units in the astral body, and seven correlating endocrine glands in the physical body. The seven major chakras and the seven corresponding endocrine glands are: crown chakra and pineal gland; third-eye chakra and pituitary gland; throat chakra and thyroid gland; heart chakra and thymus gland; solar plexus chakra and pancreas gland; regenerative chakra and gonad glands; and sacral chakra and adrenal glands. (See Figure 4.)

Each of the seven major endocrine glands secretes one or more hormones into the bloodstream, which carries them throughout the body to particular target organs. In general, the more there is of a particular hormone, the more active its target organ becomes. The activities of nearly

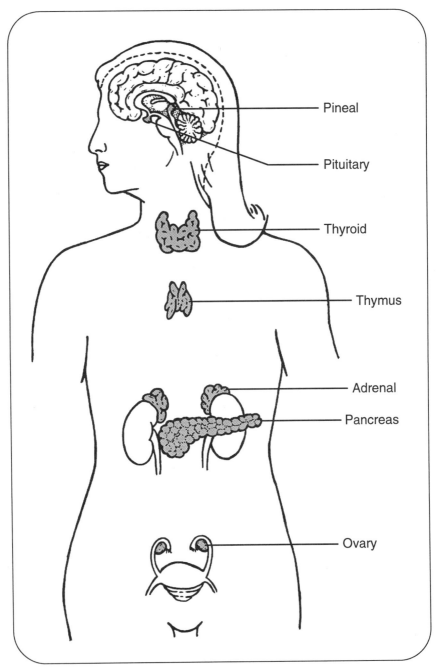

Figure 4. Endocrine glands (female).

every organ come under hormonal regulation, which produces harmony and homeostasis throughout the body. Following are the functions of the seven endocrine glands:

Pineal Gland. Scientists still are trying to delineate fully the role of this small ovoid body that is located centrally in the brain. Its main hormone probably is melatonin, which apparently regulates the cerebrum. Melatonin also regulates the hypothalamus (which governs the secretion of pituitary hormones) and the brain stem's reticular activating system (which controls the sleep-wake cycle).

Pituitary Gland. This peanut-sized organ at the base of the brain is called the master gland because it secretes nine hormones. Four of these stimulate other endocrine glands to produce their respective hormones: thyrotropin acts upon the thyroid gland; adrenocorticotropin stimulates the adrenal glands; and lutenizing hormone and follicle-stimulating hormone act upon the gonads.

The five other pituitary hormones and their functions are: growth hormone regulates the growth of the body; antidiuretic hormone acts on the kidneys to regulate urine excretion; melanocyte-stimulating hormone increases the production of pigment cells in the skin; oxytocin causes contractions of the womb in childbirth; and prolactin stimulates the breast to produce milk.

A biofeedback system governs the release of pituitary hormones. For example, when the master gland secretes thyrotropin, it causes the thyroid gland to secrete more of its hormone. When thyroid hormone reaches the desired level in the blood, the pituitary notes this and secretes less thyrotropin, thereby stabilizing or lowering thyroid activity. The hypothalamus also influences the timing and the concentration of pituitary hormonal secretions (see page 163). The pituitary serves as a wise judge that carefully weighs all of this complex information, and then secretes the needed amount of its nine hormones at the proper time.

Pituitary disorders are relatively rare. They often involve tumors that cause too much or too little production of pituitary hormones. Excessive growth hormone in children leads to gigantism, whereas insufficient growth hormone results in dwarfism. Pituitary disorders may cause imbalances in the thyroid, the adrenal and the gonad glands.

Thyroid Gland. Positioned in the neck, this gland secretes thyroxine, which regulates the metabolic rate of the body. Too much thyroxine (hyperthyroidism) may cause increased appetite, weight loss, rapid heart rate, tremor, increased nervous irritability, and hot, flushed skin. Insufficient thyroxine (hypothyroidism) may cause lethargy, intolerance to cold, weight gain and depression.

Attached to the back of the thyroid gland are four or five small parathyroid glands that secrete parathyroid hormone, which controls the concentration of calcium in the blood.

Thymus Gland. Located in front of and above the heart, this gland secretes thymosin and other hormones that regulate the lymphocytes of the immune system. Known thymic disorders are rare.

Pancreas Gland. Situated behind the stomach, the pancreas has a dual function. As a digestive organ, it produces enzymes that help to digest food. In its endocrine role, it secretes insulin and glucagon, which regulate blood sugar.

Diabetes mellitus, or high blood sugar, is the most common of all endocrine disorders. Type 1 diabetes occurs mainly in young people, when the pancreas stops producing insulin. Type 2 diabetes usually affects people over forty whose insulin output is insufficient for the body's needs.

Gonad Glands. These are the testes in the male and the ovaries in the female, which are both reproductive organs and endocrine glands. The testes secrete testosterone, whereas the ovaries secrete estrogen and progesterone. These hormones regulate the growth and the activity of the reproductive organs, and also give the body its distinctive male or female characteristics. An excess or a deficiency of gonadal hormones may cause infertility, delayed or premature puberty, failure to menstruate in the female, and development of inappropriate gender characteristics.

Adrenal Glands. Located atop the kidneys, these glands produce steroid hormones: aldosterone regulates salt concentration in the blood; hydrocortisone helps the body to respond to physical stress; and small amounts of the sex hormones augment the hormones secreted by the gonads. The adrenals also secrete epinephrine (adrenaline) and norepinephrine, which produce the same effects as stimulation by sympathetic nerves. Adrenal disorders include Addison's disease, Cushing's syndrome, and aldosteronism.

Given the complexity of the endocrine system, blood tests that measure the amount of circulating hormones, as well as other medical exams, usually are required to diagnose endocrine disorders. Hormonal supplements and other medications may be essential parts of treatment. To bring about a full healing, however, consider how mental, emotional and soul-astral difficulties with the spiritual quality of wisdom–justice–judgment may have caused the endocrine imbalance. Wisely balance the scales of justice and the endocrine dysfunction will disappear.

COLOR VISUALIZATION
Green

The green of grass and evergreen trees is the color to balance the third-eye region and the pituitary gland. When seeking healing, balance, harmony, justice for any condition or problem, flood the forehead with green.

Think of the forehead as a television tube which broadcasts its picture to the rest of the body. Remember, from the all-seeing eye and the pituitary gland, every other spiritual center and every endocrine gland of the physical system receives the image.

Use green. Walk barefoot on grass. Hike through a peaceful park. Dig in a garden or work with houseplants. Eat green leafy vegetables or suck on mint leaves, mentally seeing the chlorophyll "photosynthesizing," through the white light of the Son-light of the I Am Self, in every cell of the vehicle. Wear a green scarf around the head.

If resting or meditating, wet a soft green cloth and lay it across the forehead. Imagine clear green light-liquid soaking down through the third eye into the pituitary gland. The master gland carries it to the rest of the body, bringing balance, harmony and justice. Thus the wise domain of the I Am Self prevails over all conditions and persons in your life.

SONG INSPIRATION
Wisdom

Give me the wisdom of Solomon,
So that in my earthly kingdom Thy will may be done.
Kindle that inner light;
Shine it on what's true and right.
Give me the wisdom of Solomon.

57

Let me judge in harmony with divine law.
Let me see that justice is served for the highest good of all.
Give me inner knowing when imbalances start showing.
Let me judge in harmony with divine law.

Let me see that every day is judgment day,
Not just some dreaded event so far away.
Let me see the right for each apparent wrong,
In every thought and action my whole life long.
Let me see that every day is judgment day.

5. Will

Metaphysical Interpretation: *Matthew*

Physical Data: *Respiratory System*

Color Visualization: *Sky Blue*

Song Inspiration: *Will*

METAPHYSICAL INTERPRETATION
Matthew

Freewill choice is a primary gift of our Father-Mother God to each of Its personalized, individual beings. Moreover, it is a recurring contract of faith and trust in our Parent-Creator which we seem to repeat at each new level of growth, with each new challenge or problem we confront in our I Am unfolding.

It is our first positive performance as an infant emerging from the safety and the protection of our mother's womb. It is our first voluntary decision or will to live separately and independently from our parent-creator. The mortal part of us, like the spiritual part, never actually can be totally separate from our Creator, since we are made in the image, the likeness, the pattern, the form, the substance of our Parent-God. But in our formation stages we are totally dependent on the life-giving functions of our parent. The first thing we do of our own volition—our first freewill action—is to breathe through our own apparatus (the respiratory system) the air of this new environment. Those who refuse to breathe are stillborn. Will, therefore, relates to air in this embryonic development of the Christ Self. We must will air.

The letter W for *will* forms two inverted triangles. Descending from the Creative Force of our Father-Mother God, we enter into manifested form. Ascending from this point of individualized form, we must will to return to the Creative Force from which we originated. This is the involution into third dimensional frequency matter and the evolution back into fourth dimensional structure or I Am beingness.

Since will is the first independent action of the individualized spiritual Self, we must express this will repeatedly at various steps in our growth and development into total I Am expression as a full Christed being. To prove this point, we use Jesus of Nazareth again as our perfect example. Review how many times and in how many situations he expressed consciously that his personal, mortal will was to be one with the higher, divine will of the I Am Self.

His first challenge as an independent, free mortal was at twelve years of age in the Temple of Jerusalem. Twelve generally was accepted as the age of decision and the beginning of adulthood. So, although his mortal parents were returning to their home in Nazareth, he chose to lag behind and to serve his spiritual Parent, God, by conversing with, and challenging the ideas of, the learned rabbis in the Temple. When Mary scolded him, he replied, "Why do you scold me? Do you not know I was about my Father's business?"

Later, when he asked John the Baptist to bless him, the prophet at first refused, saying that Jesus was more worthy than he; in fact, he should be baptized by Jesus, the Messiah. Jesus could have been flattered by and have accepted this compliment; it was the truth. Instead he answered, "It is the will of my Father; and it is the proper order of events that you baptize me first." Then the I Am Self could say, "Here is my son in whom I Am well pleased."

The next challenge to Jesus was a series of battles of the mortal will versus the spiritual will, the temptations in the wilderness. These are the temptations of the soul in the wilderness of this alien and mortal environment, plus the weaknesses of the flesh body. Jesus played out the problems, the heartaches, the questions, the confusions which beset any spiritual teacher or leader on Earth. He was presented with a choice: spiritual thoughts and actions, or immediate but temporary glory and acclaim. Jesus never was forced to play the role of spiritual teacher and messiah. He freely chose the opportunities presented to him by time, circumstances and divine revelations.

Moreover, he never was given the whole drama, the entire picture and all of the consequences resulting from these decisions, at any given moment. It was a constantly unfolding, gradual, step-by-step realization; as it is to all who are evolving back into their spiritual, child-of-God status. At each challenge, with each step forward, Jesus had to make his own freewill choice to accept what was presented, to ignore it and thus to stand still (be stillborn), or to retreat or in effect to go backwards into deeper human involvement and karma.

Each of Jesus' demonstrations as a Christed being likewise was a choice of his free will: the various healings, the transfiguration on the mount for three of his apostles, the walking on water, the changing of water into wine, the feeding of the five thousand, the giving of teachings and prophecies for the next two thousand years of Earthman's evolution, and so forth. None of these conscious acts were forced upon him; nor were they inevitable, beyond his control. Only Judas the betrayer forced his hand, and even then Jesus permitted the betrayal to take its course.

At each new step of our growth, at each new challenge or problem in the developing state of Christhood, we may move forward, stand still, or go backwards, any of these three courses according to our free will.

The greatest decision is at the total crucifixion of the mortal life for the spiritual one. Knowing that death would come of Judas' betrayal, Jesus prayed in Gethsemane* for further illumination, guidance, clarity, strength; but, above all, for God's will to be done through him. Until his actual expiration (breathing out for the last time), Jesus still was making freewill choices as to how far and how long he might carry Spirit's resolve and desire to demonstrate the resurrection of the flesh and the dissolving of the myth that man had created, the so-called death.

He continued to demonstrate free will during the three dark days in the tomb. For during that stage of his transformation, Jesus the man and the Christ/Father/Self within acted as one. The Father's will was the son's will. He and the Father within were one will and one expression: I am that I Am.

Therefore, in our mortal personality growth into the full expression of the I Am Self in embodiment, we also must demonstrate that act of willing—regardless of costs, pain, disillusionment, misunderstandings, betrayals, hatreds, our own fears—to bring the mortal will into at-one-ment with the spiritual will of our divine Self.

The demonstration does not get necessarily easier, either. For with each new stage of unfoldment the tasks become more difficult, the responsibilities more serious, the challenges and possible failures greater. When we are embryonic in form, the parent-mother takes care of all decisions and needs. When we are little children, both parents aid in helping us make decisions, particularly where the consequences are unknown to our limited experiences in this environment. But as we become adult and are given opportunities of power in co-creator functions and responsibilities as children of God our Parent, our freewill choices have long-range, serious consequences; but, at the same time, opportunities for service and glory.

On the mortal level, our will aspect can be self-defeating. This is shown in the drama of Jesus wherein the disciple Levi, son of Alphaeus, was a taxgatherer. Until that one is called by the Christ Self (Jesus) to follow him, he is engaged in gathering up substance and livelihood from the leftovers, the taxes of all the other citizens in the nation or personality expression. Levi means *a unifier, one who gathers or binds things up for another.* Alphaeus means *a chief or a leader, a supplanter who represents another higher than himself.*

---

* Gethsemane: metaphysically, to press out all errors and to leave only truth.

When this mortal expression willingly follows the higher Self, he transforms into Matthew: *a gift of Yahweh (I Am); one who gives wholly to the I Am being.* Charles Fillmore in the *Metaphysical Bible Dictionary* stated for the aspect of Matthew, "When the individual will has become a disciple of the Christ, spiritual I Am, the schooling of the man begins." Thus it follows that after the four cornerstones—faith, strength, love, wisdom—have been laid to build (birth) the light body/temple, the mortal self must consciously express its willingness for, then be schooled methodically by the Father-Mother God as to, his role and mission as one of His-Her children.

The most flagrant abuse of free will comes through Judas, representative in the I Am for the regenerative life force. Judas made his freewill choice; though he later did regret that choice and tried to stop the sequence of events which inevitably followed his act. But the I Am (Jesus), for its own higher purposes, permitted (willed) him to follow through; to show dynamically and without question what consequences would result from those choices.

Isn't it interesting that when the drama or the effect of that freewill choice was concluded, the remaining eleven apostles were obligated to replace Judas with another disciple, named Matthias? The name Matthias is a derivative of Matthew, the disciple of spiritual will. Self-will of the mortal, abuse of will through Judas, resulted in reinforcement by another who represents divine will being done.

The most frequently asked question by students of spiritual life is: what is God's will? Since God is good, God's will is good for all that is involved in the condition. God is synonymous with cosmic (good) laws in action: harmony, justice, peace, love; proper thinking, speaking and acting toward one and all.

Thus, when there are strife, anxiety, fear, worry and rage there can be no divine will involved. For these conditions are the antitheses of what God's will is for His-Her creations. These are the symptoms of mortal, temporary self-will in operation. It is not so much that these conditions are sins in themselves but that they are signals that our mortal wills are superseding what divine will desires for us. Never can there be proper fulfillment until spiritual will dominates the individual, mortal, self-centered will of the human part of our nature. Thus the will aspect is the pivotal action, the most complex and the most involved, of all the twelve characteristics of the Christ Self.

Although it is free and seemingly independent and individual, nevertheless will is the quality which creates more interdependence and responsibility to others than any of the other qualities. In our freedom to choose, we are obligated to be responsible for many unseen and unknown acts and associates in future development.

It may be put this way. At the moment the newborn chooses to live or not to live in that body, his choice has an immediate effect upon the parents, their lives and future decisions, relatives, friends; in fact, upon the whole sociological structure in which all of them live. If the child chooses to breathe and to live, there will be adjustments, sacrifices and obligations, as well as many joys, pleasures, sharings, fulfillments of hopes and desires on the part of all with whom that individual comes into contact during his life span.

If the individual chooses not to breathe, not to live at that time and through that body prepared for him by the parents, there still are enormous adjustments, emotional reactions, responsibilities of others; conditions which ensue through the parents, family, associates, and society in general. There also are unknown and countless decisions and activities which the soul (and those connected with him) must resolve in other realms of existence in order to adjust to that decision not to participate physically in that given time and place.

Now consider how much more is involved if a spiritual worker or leader makes the wrong choice. This could be by wrong teachings and ideas, wrong messages and information, wrong motives and actions. The implications are vast, because the sphere of influence of a spiritual teacher is considerably more vast than for those who have only average consciousness and responsibilities within the race evolvement. When righteous action is inaugurated, a chain of circumstances is boundless; and equally so when evil, self-serving, careless, ignorant, noncaring thoughts, teachings or deeds are performed by those with spiritual force behind them. Unimaginable damages are triggered in a chain of seemingly endless circumstances.

Suppose Jesus, at any point in his ministry, had made the freewill choice not to continue. Let your thoughts unfold as to what might have transpired to each individual of that time and place. What would have been the history of man on this planet?

When Mary asked Jesus to change the water into wine at the wedding feast in Cana, suppose he had said, "It is not my time and I do not want to take further responsibility." This was his first, mortal reaction to his mother's request. But something higher superseded and made him change his mind. Suppose, challenged and thwarted by all kinds of learned authorities, he had just given up and said, "That's it. I've had it. This is the end of the line. Good-bye." Suppose that in Gethsemane he had decided to flee, or to go underground with his teachings, or to forget the revelation that he as the Messiah was to vanquish man's mortal and last enemy: so-called death.

How many lives, how many generations would his wrong decisions have affected; how many families, future commitments, societies, nations; in fact, the whole evolutionary progression of man's return unto his rightful condition and understanding of his status as a child of the Father-Mother Creator?

While implanting the will-of-God quality in order to anchor the light body fully into the third dimensional body, each spiritual worker must weigh the consequences of his freewill choices: choose *for* challenges, problems, conditionings, changes, pains, doubts and unknown functions of that light-body form, or choose *against* such. Whatever blossoms from our choice, we each must be ready to reap those consequences to ourselves individually, to our presently established society, to the race as a whole.

Before we may assume spiritual power and mastership over all other kingdoms and species—which are the natural consequences of the receptive, responsive, alternating side of our spiritual-will characteristic (see the following chapter)—we must implant the proper spiritual will firmly and unequivocally through every thought, word and deed. There is enough evidence everywhere on Earth to demonstrate what the selfish, error, limited, mortal type of will can do in wreaking havoc throughout the other kingdoms. Spiritual powers can come only as a partner aspect to that of spiritual will. The former depends on the latter. The proper spiritual will expresses only when the individual's mortal thinking, saying and believing accept totally: "Not my will be done, but Thy will through me as Your instrument."

Releasing the self-centered, mortal will is not easy. It takes more than intellectual logic and well-intended platitudes. The will to release this free gift of God to each of His children is monumental, extraordinarily complex; and requires strict discipline of the self, all the mortal energies combined. This takes an extremely dedicated and strong individual.

Spiritual workers especially are called upon now, in this present age of marks and demonstrations, to show man of Earth how to release his mortal-will gift to the higher one, to think in terms of, "The will of my I

Am Self be done through me." If those in the advance guard do not demonstrate submission to divine will, each one in his own sphere of influence and in his particular role and mission, it will make it unbelievably difficult for others to desire, to experience, and actually to release themselves to, the higher Self. The race moves together as a whole species. Individuals may pioneer the path into the fourth dimensional frequency, but they do not evolve separately and independently from the whole. We interact on one another exactly as the cells of our own bodies do.

Just as the cells of our bodies make up the citizens of our personal I Am nation, so the citizens of Earth make up the cells in the body of the cosmic Christ, the Son-of-God creation. Each single cell/citizen has an effect on the whole, just as the whole evolutionary pattern has an effect on each one of its parts.

As each one relinquishes selfish interests, mortal will, self-serving desires to those ideals of the higher vibration—the I Am will for the good of all equally—the spiritual energy and purpose raise all simultaneously. Without this shift of attention, which is energy, from mortal and personal will into immortal and spiritual will, the desired sequence of events cannot occur. Here is the evolution of our son-of-man pattern (spiritual being in animal form) back to Son-of-God status and powers (spiritual being in I Am, light-body form). Jesus with his twelve apostles (characteristics of the Christ) firmly set this evolutionary pattern. There is no possible way of changing the pattern or creating a separate path on this particular planet.

It was no accident, nor should it be overlooked for the symbolism intended, that Jesus selected a tax collector, Matthew, to portray the will quality of the Son of God, Christed man. The tax collector takes only a percentage of the total substance and earnings from the citizens of the nation. The tax collector is a representative of the one who rules the land (the body of the individual).

Whether the ruler is righteous or malicious more or less depends on the consciousness and the karma of the group being ruled. So it is in our own bodies that our conscious mind (ruler) is just or unjust, sane or mad, fair-minded or tyrannical. Our thoughts and desires constitute the type of conscious mind (ruler) we are over ourselves and our affairs. If the ruler becomes too unruly, it is up to the collective citizens/cells of that nation/body to repent and to replace him.

The tax collected from all the citizens is supposed to be used to keep law and order within the whole nation/body. When the ruler (conscious mind) is governed by the I Am, the order is just and fair to each of the citizens/cells equally. Only from the I Am consciousness can one understand all facets of the nation in proper perspective: the mental faculties and perceptions, the physical requirements and opportunities, the soul responsibilities and cleansings, the emotional development and expressions. Therefore, from this elevated viewpoint of the I Am Self, the percentage of tax extracted from each cell/citizen is right and good, proper and pure. From this correct percentage—the tithing principle—of spiritual law, order and harmony, further development and future evolvement of the individual and the race grow in a graceful manner.

Even from the most crass, materialistic, mortal viewpoint it is obvious that the ruler and his representative, the tax collector, would be foolish to tax the citizens/cells beyond their resources. Taking more than a rightful share, or of the ability to give without undue strain, eventually must result in drying up the very source itself. The cosmic view sees this clearly. The mortal view often is blinded and cannot see beyond its momentary, temporary lust. Mortal man time and time again has killed the goose that lays the golden egg; has cut off his own nose to spite his face.

Therefore, to rise up to spiritual thinking we must recognize there is a just and correct duty to be paid to the I Am Self. Freely we must give a percentage of our energy, thoughts, desires to the higher Self. This duty or tax becomes the leavening in the bread; a term Jesus used allegorically to represent our physical bodies or forms. The leavening or tax raises the whole. It serves the basic needs required to govern the whole being. This spiritual will or tax is spread throughout the land/body and acts to serve those other parts which as yet have not become enlightened enough, or have not energy and spiritual dedication enough, to serve the ruler, the I Am Self.

The I Am Self, a wise judge and master over all aspects of our being, raises each part of its kingdom so that all are in proper harmony and have equal portions of the energy/supply. The I Am Self is right-acting and discerns spiritually or wholly; therefore, it knows what is best for the total being (physical, mental, emotional, soul-psychic aspects). It takes the taxes/tithes from those who have supply, and equalizes them with the needs of those who have not sufficient supply.

Remember that cosmic truth serves on every level. Therefore, when the Hierarchy of this solar system planned this present evolutionary program to raise all men of Earth from third dimensional form into fourth dimensional, light-body form, the ascended masters instructed Mark-

Age to help enlighten and raise one hundred and forty-four thousand program workers to work for this Second Coming. The Second Coming is not only the return of the light body to man of Earth but also the return of the spiritual ruler, the I Am pattern maker, he who was last known as Christ Jesus.

Those one hundred and forty-four thousand individuals comprise only a small percentage, a symbolic as well as a literal tax or duty, to serve the five and a half billion souls incarnated on the planet, plus those untold millions or billions who affect the Earth through their astral connections and influences. When the one hundred and forty-four thousand light workers consciously are working for the I Am Nation of enlightened souls on Earth and in the astral, they will be able to leaven or to raise the whole race. Their lights will enlighten those who have not the light, the truth, the way of spiritual thoughts, desires, motives and plans.

Remember, too, that this cosmic pattern of truth is similar in our personal body/nation, in that there are one hundred and forty-four thousand spiritual centers in the brain which, when infused with light, transmit it to all the other parts of the brain. This light then automatically sparks all cells to function at the same higher frequency; the fourth dimensional, spiritual level of consciousness and service. This is to say that since the cerebrum of the brain is the central computer station for the entire body, those one hundred and forty-four thousand spiritual centers automatically trigger a chain reaction that spiritualizes all functions, concepts and abilities of the individual's functioning on all levels.

Thus, through this cosmic principle, exampling on multiple levels and for myriad purposes, we recall now that it is not necessary to transmute each thought, each aspect of our mortal will, each cell of our physical body, each experience within the total soul record of unknown numbers of incarnations, in order for us to raise our entire expression (body, mind and soul) into the I Am, light-body expression. A tax collector, the will quality in us which desires to be a child of God instead of a child of man, is sufficient to raise and to assist all our lower thought forms and conditions.

Will to be and will to do the work of the I Am ruler. Even if you do not know fully or understand yet the will in each situation, demand that the conscious mind be governed by the will of the I Am Self in all matters, ideas and situations. Rest securely in the knowledge that this token taxing of the will nature serves the entire being. The I Am Self, a just and righteous governor, does the rest for all parts of itself equally, harmoniously and in the proper sequence and time. Through the will characteristic of the I Am Self, all parts will be as one in the one consciousness.

PHYSICAL DATA
Respiratory System

The spiritual quality of will externalizes via the throat chakra as the respiratory system, which includes the nasal cavity, the sinuses, the pharynx (throat), the larynx (voice box), the trachea (windpipe), two bronchi and two lungs. (See Figure 5.) The respiratory system brings oxygen into the body and removes carbon dioxide from it.

With inspiration, oxygen-laden air passes through the nose's two nostrils and enters the nasal cavity, which is located over the roof of the mouth. The sinuses are air-filled cavities in the bones behind and above the nose. Four pairs of sinuses—frontal, maxillary, ethmoidal and sphenoidal—open via small passageways into the nasal cavity. The sinuses and the nasal cavity warm, moisten and filter the air as it travels through them.

The air then flows through the pharynx, the larynx and the trachea. The trachea divides into two tubes called bronchi, each of which carries air into one lung. In the lungs, the bronchi divide into increasingly smaller air passages called bronchioles. At the end of the smallest bronchioles are clusters of tiny air sacs or alveoli. The lungs contain an estimated three hundred million alveoli.

Oxygen is the spark of life. In the alveoli, oxygen diffuses through the alveolar walls into the surrounding blood, which carries it to every part of the body. Oxygen diffuses from the blood into the cells, where it combines with glucose (sugar) to produce heat and the energy that powers all cellular activities. The waste product of this reaction is carbon dioxide, which diffuses from the cells into the blood. The blood transports the carbon dioxide to the lungs where it diffuses into the alveoli. With expiration, carbon-dioxide-rich air travels via the respiratory tract to the nose, where it is expelled from the body.

Soul-astral, emotional and mental imbalances of the will characteristic may be the principal or a contributing cause of the following and other respiratory disorders: the common cold; the flu; allergic rhinitis (hay fever); sinusitis (inflammation of the sinuses); bronchitis (inflammation of the bronchi); asthma (partial obstruction of the bronchi and

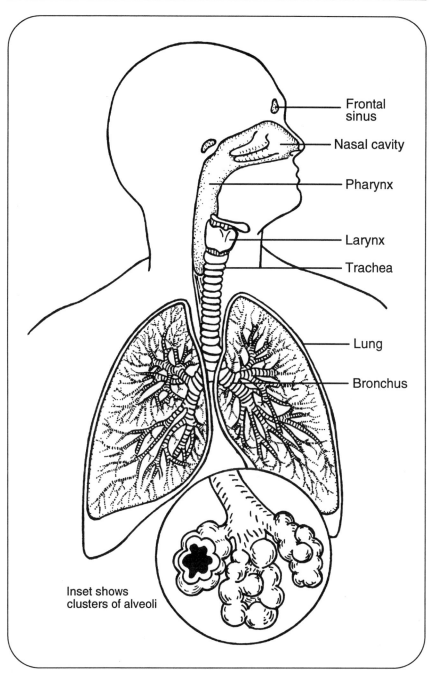

Frontal
sinus

Nasal cavity

Pharynx

Larynx

Trachea

Lung

Bronchus

Inset shows
clusters of alveoli

Figure 5. Respiratory system.

bronchioles due to contraction of the muscles in the bronchial walls); emphysema (damage to the alveoli and decreased elasticity in the lung); pneumonia (inflammation of the lungs); tuberculosis; pleurisy (inflammation of the pleura or lining around the lungs); and lung cancer (which almost always is caused by lung damage from smoking).

God's will for all His-Her children is harmony, wholeness and health. Therefore, when there is a respiratory disorder, mentally breathe in God's will. Align your mortal will with His divine will. Consult with family, friends, physicians, counselors or spiritual teachers who can help you uncover and transmute soul-emotional imbalances that are causing or contributing to your respiratory disease. Take whatever physical remedy or apply any physical treatment that promotes your healing, including medication, nutritional supplements, breathing exercises or surgery. In Spirit's time, your respiratory system will manifest vibrant health.

COLOR VISUALIZATION
Sky Blue

It should not be difficult to imagine and to breathe in sky blue for air, for heaven, for God's will in every thought, word and deed. Use the most popular analogies and images of vast expanses of space. There is no place on Earth where we cannot look up and see, feel, breathe in, encase ourselves in the sky blue of air as a life-giving substance.

Dwell on universal symbols, to reveal your personal struggles concerning mortal will versus spiritual will. How do ominous clouds, thunder, lightning, heavy winds represent various stages of your self-will? How do sunlight and warm air disperse those storms which frighten and damage?

Infinite, sky-blue heaven is the will of God through us as mortal beings. This is our ceiling. It is eternal. The air itself is a garment, an aura as expansive as the imagination can reach. Breathe in this sky blue as you would breathe only divine consciousness and spiritual desires into every pore of the body/nation which you are. The air is in you. You are in the air.

Relax totally: mind, body and soul. Awake or asleep, automatically you are breathing in air, I Am. The air is free, as the will of God is free. The air is God's will cleansing, purifying, transmuting, keeping you alive in Him . . . I'mm . . . Mmm . . . Omm!

SONG INSPIRATION
Will

Thy will only,
Thy will be done.
My life I live
To serve the One.
To do Thy will
I will, I will.
I live to see
Thy will be done.

Let me know what I am to do.
Give me the strength to see it through.
Let me begin to do Thy will.
Thy will be mine.
Thy will I will.

I breathe Thy will.
I choose Thy will.
Thou art my breath.
Thou art my skill.

Guide me to know,
Each time I decide,
What is Your will.
Let it be my guide.
Thy will only,
Thy will be done.
I live to see
Thy will be done.

6. Power

Metaphysical Interpretation: *Philip*

Physical Data: *Larynx, Muscles & Limbs*

Color Visualization: *Deep Aqua*

Song Inspiration: *Power*

METAPHYSICAL INTERPRETATION
Philip

Spiritual power, mastery on the physical of the cosmic laws, conscious governance on Earth over all the other kingdoms can come only after special dedication, understanding and blending of the five previous spiritual characteristics of the I Am Self. When we have implanted properly the spiritual characteristic of power into our thoughts, words and actions, we have completed the first half of the anchoring of the light body through the physical vessel.

The first six characteristics are known in the Old Testament as the gifts or the dowry of Yahweh. Since the six are three pairs of active-receptive principles of the Lord, they represent the involution of the Trinity of God into manifested form or individualization; as we know and call it, the I Am Self expression. The Trinity of God is symbolized by an equilateral triangle pointing downward. The pairs are: faith and strength (the Father aspect), love and wisdom (the Mother aspect), will and power (the Son or Christ in manifested form).

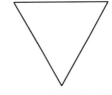

Involution of Trinity of God

The trinity of man in his Christ or Son-of-God aspect, symbolized by the equilateral triangle pointing upwards, is the evolution of man back to the infinite Source of being. This trinity also acts in three pairs or six specific characteristics of the I Am being: imagination and understanding (the spiritual-mental faculties), order and zeal (the soul-emotional faculties), regeneration and elimination (the physical-body form).

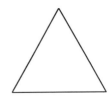

Evolution of trinity of man

When we have implanted all twelve characteristics (apostles) of our individualized I Am Self, the Son-of-God being each of us truly is, we will begin to demonstrate

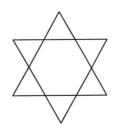

Star of David

through the light body our inherent spiritual talents and functions. That unification of our dual nature (immortal involuting into matter, with the

77

mortal evolving out of matter back into spiritual, light-body form) is symbolized by the six-pointed Star of David. With their active-receptive qualities or polarities, the six points comprise twelve houses or tribes; which are all the tools of our Christ Self in the light body, born into matter as the Son of God manifested through the son of mankind. (See the following table.)

IMPLANTING 12 CHARACTERISTICS OF I AM SELF

Trinity Action	Active Polarity	Receptive Polarity
Involution ▽ Trinity of God	Faith	Strength
	Love	Wisdom
	Will	Power
Evolution △ Trinity of Man	Imagination	Understanding
	Order	Zeal
	Regeneration	Elimination

The ancients understood that spiritual power is the proper blending and coordination, the unity, of all divine forces. They expressed this in symbols, myth and legend, allegory. In the passage of time, many of these symbols have been misinterpreted, misunderstood and wrongly applied. To portray the power of God in man, the ancients used three symbols: the centaur, the sword, and the speaking of the word. In the New Testament, the apostle Philip represents the power aspect of the Christ personality, Jesus. The name Philip literally means *lover of horses*; metaphysically interpreted: *one who loves and properly uses spiritual power.*

The centaur—with head, shoulders, arms and hands of a man, combined with the lower body of a horse—was used in mythology to represent that the power of a spiritual being has the mind and the consciousness of man by the strength and the manipulative creativeness which only can be expressed by shoulders, arms and hands; plus the speed, the beauty, the sheer physical energy of animal force as a horse.

The horse was ancient man's fastest mode of transportation. It allowed man to conquer and to have power over all terrain, including over other animals, such as hunting them for food; and it assisted man in agricultural and self-protecting pursuits. So, combining the extremities with their muscular functions and the brain, with the mental capacities of man, the centaur aptly represented spiritual powers in the highest, most exemplary physical manner.

Whether riding for pleasure, hunting or in any form of livelihood, expert riders strive to blend with the horse. The two become as one. Their minds lock, even exchange thoughts. Their two bodies interact with one another; each knowing the power, the weight, the weaknesses and the needs of the other. This union of mind and body, symbolized by the centaur, never was intended to infer that spiritual man was part animal, but that he was to use his physical form with the wisdom and the guidance of his higher spiritual knowledge and instincts.

It also was intended to convey the message that spiritual man can unite with the power and the energy of physical animal force for the good of that form which he is using, to have right and proper dominion over all other species and elements of Earth. Spiritual power used with wisdom, justice, faith and the will of God will not disrupt, harm, abuse or destroy other creations of the One Source, Spirit, from which we all derive our forms. Therefore, when this characteristic of our I Am Self comes forth it automatically is tempered with the divine conscience. There is no selfish motivation. There is no advantage taken. There is no domination whereby one creature benefits more than the other.

Power also frequently is represented by the two-edged sword. The lessons learned from this symbol are no less significant or interesting than those gained from the horse or the centaur. The two-edged sword conveys that when we use our spiritual powers, whatever we have used upon others can be turned and used upon us. It is a caution: if we use power on any level, we should expect it to be used upon us in equal measure. In the modern vernacular: if you can't take it, don't dish it out.

The motive and the methods employed must be of the highest level of consciousness, the I Am Self. Otherwise, that two-edged sword will cut and will maim the very body it is supposed to be protecting. There is no need to fear this sword, provided one's conscience is perfectly clear and contains no hidden, self-propelling motives.

To carry this analogy further, the governor of all aspects and forms of the Earth domain must use the cutting sword with spiritual discernment and proper judgment, considering the highest good of each of its parts before wielding this instrument of power. Similarly, the surgeon does not operate on a vital organ of the body if the other organs are not healthy enough to support the procedure.

Power arouses suspicion and fear among those who are unenlightened or who are in less than absolute control of their other Christ characteristics. And well it should, for power carries with it an awesome responsibility. But often we learn the lessons of the I Am on the physical dimension through trial and error. So, if we are willing, honest, earnest students of these divine characteristics of our spiritual heritage, we must be receptive to experimenting with the various stages, with the varying levels and feelings of different kinds, of power which enter into our lives. We really cannot avoid them, nor can we afford to ignore this part of our divine heritage.

According to cosmic law, we use power and are used by power. Thus, we must learn everything we can about this two-way street; this two-edged, dangerous but useful instrument. Those who use power without first learning the lessons of faith–strength, love–wisdom and power's partner, will, in the long run shall suffer more through the law of cause and effect than the ones upon whom power is wielded. "The meek shall inherit the Earth" means that those who are patient and trust in the divine law of cause and effect know this aspect of the two-edged sword.

In our eternal experiencing, growing, evolving to and becoming the I Am Self in action, the lessons learned, even through the misuse of power, become valuable and important. Some are negative lessons of power, but even those are imprinted on the soul memory for positive purposes. They result in deep impression, with proper respect for the cosmic laws, for our responsibilities as masters of these laws, for our functions as governors over all dominions, for the vast potential at our command as manipulators of energy.

Furthermore, in this analogy the sword is the weapon for truth, which is divine law in action. To wield the sword of truth—to hold it and to put it to use properly—means that man as the Son of God must have mobility, creativity, and constructive outlets for the truth. On the physical, man expresses this mobility through the arms and the hands, the legs and the feet, and the entire muscular system.

Therefore, it is common, when developing the light body and feeling its connection in and through the physical form, to experience heat or tingling sensations in the extremities. The hips, the legs and the feet give us mobility, the movements necessary to carry out the spiritual laws on the physical domain. The shoulders, the arms and the hands are the manipulating, managerial aspects of our governance role as children of God on Earth.

One of the more advanced talents of spiritual power, using both the higher and the lower extremities, is a form of body language called universal sign language. In its purest form, used by Christed ones on the etheric planes, this is the manipulation of energy force fields.

Auric healing is one expression of universal sign language. The healing activity is the skillful management of energy in a person's auric field in order to remove negative soul patterns and to redistribute positive and constructive thought forms or energies through the soul and the mental bodies. Eventually from these two levels the etheric thought forms work down into the physical expression. These manipulations can affect the emotional climate of the individual and the thinking apparatus and patterns until finally the physical imperfections are dissolved.

Another purpose of the universal sign language, both on the higher planes and through purified channels on Earth, is for communication or messages from the celestial and the etheric planes. Science is just rediscovering that many animals on Earth, from the gigantic whale to the minute ant, communicate with each other through a body language. Using their individualistic forms, and considering the uniqueness of their environment, they already are masters and governors of their particular worlds. Similarly, in a higher sense, some awakened to spiritual power have learned to manipulate and to re-form energy patterns on the invisible planes. They are able to implant in the auric shield around the Earth new thought forms, ideas, codes, decrees, messages to be picked up later by those in the astral planes and to be influential factors for those living on Earth. Here, too, the body language is a form of communication. Only here it is to communicate spiritual needs, ideas, decisions, and patterns to be followed.

Many ancient societies knew and understood the power of universal sign language. This is the source of all forms of dance as we know it. Originally, dance was part of temple worship. Those practicing it were trained priests and priestesses of the divine laws. Some mystical sects— such as the Hasidim of Judaism, the Sufis of Islam, the Shakers of Protestantism—currently encourage dance and movement in order to induce ecstasy or to aid in the overshadowing of the spiritual Self. These adherents believe in and use psychic talents, and some have clairvoyant experiences. In dance, consciously or not, they are manipulating life force through the auric field which surrounds all matter form, whether of animate or inanimate nature.

Modern trends have abused these rituals and powers to such a degree that instead of accepting and developing them, some churches have gone so far as to forbid this spiritual expression, even calling it sacrilegious and pagan in nature. Nevertheless, our spiritual characteristics cannot be ruled or controlled by man-made concepts or regulations. Movement and manipulation of energy are rightful expressions of the power aspect of the I Am Self. Thus, as children of God we can manage other forces, kingdoms, life forms via wise use and spiritual knowledge.

Eventually we must return the art of dance to its proper place, when we express in our light-body forms. To consider this concept raises the question: is not every move we make, every step we take a form of power and a manipulation of energy?

Yes. When man recognizes the tremendous power of his thoughts and his body, even from the negative and somewhat unconscious or unwilling states of mind, he will become more responsible, and eager to control and to govern this. First, he must be master over himself before he is made governor over others, and eventually over all the other kingdoms in his domain. This is an awesome realization. Yet it befits the children of God descended into and involved in material form on the Earth plane. All that comes into our thoughts, words and expressions must be governed by goodness and by justice for all forms of life.

The third manner in which the children of God on Earth exercise power is through the voice. The Gospel of John begins: "When all things began, the Word already was. The Word dwelt with God, and what God was, the Word was. The Word, then, was with God at the beginning, and through it all things came to be; no single thing was created without it. All that came to be was alive with its life, and that life was the light of men. The light shines on in the dark, and the darkness has never mastered it."

The *word* is the thought, the ideas of God. The Mother aspect of God brings it into manifestation. The Son is the manifestation of the word. As children of this triune Parent, we must follow the pattern. We express power in this sense through our voice equipment, especially the larynx. By inhaling and exhaling air (the will characteristic, as portrayed by the partner of power, the apostle Matthew), we create sound via the vocal cords. We make manifest the word from our I Am Selves.

On Earth, some methods we use to execute the ideas from our I Am are speaking, singing, chanting, or playing a musical instrument. These sounds release the higher energy patterns which communicate cosmic invocations, decrees, instructions and desires to the lower thought forms and patterns existing temporarily on the astral and the physical planes of life. Not only do we affect others by sound but we actually transmute conditions in our soul memory patterns, in our outer conditions and environment, in our relationships with others.

Remember, Jesus said, "If you had the faith of even a mustard seed, you would be able to *say* to that mountain, be thou removed, and it would be moved." Joshua *sounded* the trumpets and the walls of Jericho fell. There is a power in sound which modern man is only now learning; rather, relearning, remembering as he returns unto his Son-of-God status on Earth through the birth of the light body.

As there are three allegorical or mystical symbols to convey the power of God through His-Her Son, mankind, so there are three zones of power we are capable of using. There is only one Source for power: God, Creative Force. There is only one Power: God, Primal Energy. But man, made in the image and the likeness of God, is made up of a trinity: spirit-mind, soul-emotions, his body. Saying there are various zones of utilizing this one Power confuses the unenlightened into believing there is more than one Source, or that the power of the sons of man is un-related to the power of the sons of God.

First and foremost, consider the spiritual-mental power of the I Am Self. This is not all the power of the universe, nor all of God's Energy, but is a single, individualized part of the Source, created by our Father-Mother Parent. In this zone of expression there is a total and equal blending of all areas of our being.

In the second zone, the individual predominantly expresses astral memories, past karma, emotional reactions. These often are simply sub-conscious responses due to a series of experiences not consciously con-trolled, analyzed or understood. In this realm there can be dynamic demonstrations, awe-inspiring to some, of the psychic talents inherent in every one of us.

These psychic talents are part of our I Am heritage; but usually the majority on Earth utilize them without conscious control, understanding, or the highest of spiritual motivations. In fact, we must recognize that if we use psychic powers without concomitant spiritual development and light-body anchoring, we cannot possibly take into consideration the celestial and the etheric levels that govern the evolution of the sons of man back into Son-of-God status.

Psychic power used for its own sake usually is an outlet for vanity, self-glory, personal attention, and a desire to command others. These others may be astral forces or entities who are willing to reply to questions and to give guidance regarding the physical zone of life. Those operating from a strictly psychic zone of activity are not interested in, nor are they capable of understanding, the person's spiritual evolvement to the I Am Self.

The sphere of influence from the psychic-astral-soul level is limited. This zone can clear up conditions for a few persons. Due to the very nature and the limitations of its orbit, it cannot possibly resolve and balance all conditions, forces, and forms of matter, because it cannot influence the zone above its own frequency range. But there is no question that those operating from the astral-soul-psychic-emotional areas can and do influence individuals and creative forms and forces within their ranges and on the one below them, which is the physical, Earth plane. Thus this zone can be fraught with danger and foolishness, because the comprehension and the dedication of those involved are limited.

On the other hand, we need not shun or fear psychic powers. Jesus demonstrated these ESP qualities (Elementary Spiritual Powers) innumerable times throughout his ministry. Most of his healings involved only a few individuals and their families. He read the soul history of the Samaritan woman at the well. This demonstration only influenced a small number: the woman herself and a few townspeople.

Psychic power, which is the ability to tune in to the soul records of individuals and groups, can be good, helpful, even necessary, on the road upward toward Christ mastery and the eventual unlocking of spiritual-mind power. But it can be tapped by the pure and the impure alike. For all of us, due to our many lifetimes, have infinite soul memories, endless experiences and talents in our memory banks or computers. Our soul journeys have resulted in a wide variety of talents and accomplishments on many planes, planets and dimensions, touching the activities and the soul plans of great numbers of individuals on those planes of living. In this respect, psychic power is far from being limited or undesirable. It has its place and purpose. However, it must never be confused with the higher spiritual power of the I Am Self, which covers a higher zone of understanding and a much broader view of man's total experiences.

Stepping down to a still lower zone of activity: physical power and mastership usually express because of selfishness and personal greed. Most often they are sought as a means of attaining a superior position over others, and through a desire to control other people and the immediate environment; or to be in a special position of prestige, according to man-made standards and values.

Yet, this zone is no less important than the higher two zones of expression. It is necessary for mankind in his evolvement back to the Son-of-God status to learn how to master his physical body and environment. The I Am individual recognizes this, and in some ways can be more tolerant of and patient with those who exercise physical power, either rightly or wrongly.

In spite of the fact that it is the most dangerous area to play with as far as power is concerned, it is subject to the law of cause and effect as much as the other zones of activity are. Eventually all that is thought, spoken and done is returned unto the sender. It changes not; the sword (power) of truth (cosmic laws) is a two-edged sword.

Therefore, a person who is a leader in earthly, material ways and who abuses his power and position eventually faces a similar situation in which he is the one being led, or is subjected to the very abuses he perpetrated in another time and place. There is no escape from this cosmic law. Divine love and forgiveness alone can mitigate its literal and specific effects.

Contrary to some interpretations, Jesus as our Christ pattern and way shower never shunned physical leadership. But he was extremely cautious and circumspect about assuming physical powers and leadership for their sakes alone. He knew the cosmic laws better than that. He saw beyond the physical injustices and imperfections, into those zones of astral-soul problems; and, higher yet, into the spiritual-mental areas from which the decrees, the plans, the life incarnations were issued by the masters and the governors on the celestial and the etheric planes, from which he was sent to the Earth planet.

Jesus kept insisting that the kingdom of which he spoke is not of this world. Physical power or control, no matter how extensive, still can affect only a limited zone of experience and growth. As many people, lives and areas as it can affect, it still is the smallest sphere of influence of the triune levels of man's expression: spiritual-mental; astral-soul-emotional; physical body, life and personal relationships.

A physical leader, no matter how powerful or how long he or she reigns, cannot possibly control all of anyone's thoughts, ambitions, plans and schemes. No one can control another's independent, individualized thoughts (spiritual-mental zone of activity) or emotions (astral-soul memories and powers). If we needed any proof of this, Judas proved it two thousand years ago. Because of his I Am consciousness, Jesus was able to turn Judas' physical betrayal into a demonstration for the astral-soul and the spiritual-mental zones of the entire race's evolutionary development.

Spiritual power, as demonstrated by his Christ Self through Jesus, keeps a balance and a harmony with all zones of activity, with all forces on all levels of experience, with all the creative elements in those zones of expression. Only through the characterizations or the faculties of all the Christed powers can one express such a mastery over all domains. Those performances by I Am individuals thus affect the evolutionary pattern of whole species of beings, as well as the evolutionary plans of planets and solar systems.

It is obvious that spiritual power of this magnitude and from this zone of consciousness is a great rarity in the history of Earth as we now know it. But it has been demonstrated; and we are in the process of seeing it again through many more I Am individualizations, thanks to the pattern and the way shown by Jesus the Christ.

When Jesus did demonstrate the light-body powers, he selected only those to be witnesses who eventually would comprehend what the demonstration signified, and hopefully who would attempt to emulate him. Because he was in the I Am consciousness, he realized that this understanding and this desire to imitate his pattern might take as much as two thousand years of the evolutionary process. But he remained steadfast, and taught that the light-body demonstration would affect and change the entire planet and all creatures and elements connected with it. Here now is the purpose of this treatise, *Birth of the Light Body*, for this Mark Age period and program.

Walking on the water was a demonstration of the powers of the light body over the elements of the Earth. The spiritual-mental zone of man's triune being has mastership over the astral-soul-emotional and the physical forms of Earth.

Multiplying the loaves and the fishes was another demonstration of the spiritual-mental powers, despite all logic and laws of the lower areas of man's expression on Earth. It proved that those with spiritual powers of the I Am Self could supersede those in power and control over physical needs. This is an extremely dangerous stand to take, both in those days and in these times.

For those of foolish and limited comprehension who seek and achieve physical power over others—such as through the control of food and energy supplies, physical governments and man-made laws and regulations, churches that espouse dogma but not spiritual laws and truths— are directly threatened by these higher expressions of power; especially since the one wielding true spiritual power seeks no special honor, place, position or reward. Quite the contrary; the I Am individual seeks to elevate each and every one, and to balance out all injustices, partialities and privileges.

Those with motivations for power on the physical and the soul-astral-emotional spheres of influence are totally incapable of understanding the motivations of those with the spiritual-mental consciousness of the I Am and the powers that go with the light-body expression. So, they plot and scheme to overthrow what they do not understand and what they fear.

Jesus knew, understood and expected all of this. So should all who reach for and attain the I Am, light-body experiences. It is no easy time or task in this particular level of evolution on Earth.

Because of his cosmic vision and understanding, Jesus permitted his betrayal and crucifixion. Through that he demonstrated the resurrection. From his zone of spiritual-mental powers of the I Am Self, he had control and mastery over all the elements in his physical body and environment, plus the astral-soul-emotional reactions which accompany them. From the I Am state, all powers of the lesser two zones of expression were perfectly balanced and equal in his triune expression as a son of God.

Moreover, since the resurrection was demonstrated from this selfless spiritual zone of consciousness, nothing on the planet could ever be the same again. An evolutionary pattern for the sons of man was set. The elements and all species of life were established under the government of the I Am Nation to come, when a minimum of one hundred and forty-four thousand I Am beings congregate and establish themselves as the spiritual-mental rulers of both the physical and the astral environments of Earth.

Spiritual power over the other kingdoms can come only through conscientious and wise discernment concerned with the harmony and the rhythm of all other elements and kingdoms involved. Spiritual man, when using this power, cannot disrupt the balanced relationships, the evolutionary progress and the divine order within any of the other king-doms, or the purposes of all the other elements involved. From this zone, power improves, elevates, creates new and higher manifestations for the good of all who are involved in the speaking of the word. The word is law, truth, harmony, goodness, justice, righteousness.

With this fundamental base—the setting into place of the six facets or characteristics of Spirit in matter, form and individualization—where are we of Earth in our present evolvement? First, we must conquer and demonstrate power over our physical, mortal forms and personalities. Then we must take the responsibility to face the consequences of karma, both good and bad experiences, which are revealed to us through the psychic realms and the self-contemplations of our souls and emotional responses.

Our first demonstrations must be power and mastery over the ele-ments of our personal existence: body harmony and health; physical plans, life, relationships, duties, responsibilities and activities. Then we may extend our powers to assist others. For in this slow and gradual opening to higher understanding we recognize that each one and each thing in our experience is brought into our lives because of past relation-ships and emotional releases. All that we have sent out—prior to this life and memory, and during the course of this life and its myriad involve-ments—is returned unto us.

Not until we master ourselves on both the physical and the soul zones of expression may we expect to serve others through healing, counseling and teaching without inviting dire consequences to our future expe-riences and evolutionary patterns. Involving ourselves in the lives of others, before we have understood and have mastered our own physical and soul lessons, inevitably invites a like situation in our future oppor-tunities and incarnations. Those in the I Am consciousness know this. They move cautiously and speak only the truth.

The tremendous cataclysms taking place in every zone of activity on Earth today—economic, physical, health, mental peace, emotional secu-rity and satisfaction, just and equal opportunities for all—are the direct results of the misuse of power from past episodes of man's explorations here on Earth and in the astral realms during many past incarnations and evolutionary stages of growth. Man of Earth today is reaping all that he sowed in yesteryears. In our personal experiences and our impersonal roles and functions as part of the race evolvement, we each are the result of uncountable efforts to exercise our power in the past.

Therefore, before asserting physical or psychic powers, be absolutely sure of whom and what they will affect. Are you both willing and able to handle the two-edged sword of truth which you desire to display and to use, here and now? Remember, as you use it, so it will be used upon you in like intensity, measure and intentions. So be it. This is truth.

PHYSICAL DATA
Larynx, Muscles & Limbs

The spiritual quality of power externalizes via the throat chakra as the larynx or voice box, which is located in the neck between the pharynx and the trachea. (See Figure 5 on page 71.) The larynx contains two vocal cords. During inspiration, the vocal cords are relaxed and held apart, allowing air to flow freely through the larynx on its way to the lungs. During expiration, if the vocal cords are tensed and held close together, air passing over them causes them to vibrate and to produce sound waves. The throat, mouth, sinuses and nose act as resonating chambers that amplify the sound waves and add the overtones that give the voice its distinct timbre. The lips, tongue, teeth and cheeks serve as articulators that modify the vocal tone into specific speech sounds.

Mental, emotional and soul-astral difficulties in speaking the word may cause imbalances in the throat and the larynx. Pharyngitis (inflammation of the pharynx) produces a sore throat. Laryngitis (inflammation of the voice box) may lead to hoarseness or loss of the voice. Polyps, nodules or cancerous growths may develop on the vocal cords. Power problems also may manifest as speech defects.

Since the upper parts of the respiratory system serve as vocal resonators, upper respiratory disorders may alter the voice's quality. Moreover, viral and bacterial infections of both the upper and lower sections of the respiratory system often involve or spread to the larynx. Therefore, with throat and vocal disorders, it may be necessary to analyze the spiritual qualities of both will (respiratory system) and power (larynx).

The spiritual characteristic of power also expresses via the muscles and the limbs. The body has over six hundred skeletal muscles that attach to bones. (See Figure 6.) Fibrous connective tissue surrounds skeletal muscles and extends from them as tough cords or tendons, which are continuous with the fibrous covering of bones. When skeletal muscles contract, they move the bones to which they are attached by tendons.

Skeletal muscles also are called voluntary muscles, because we can

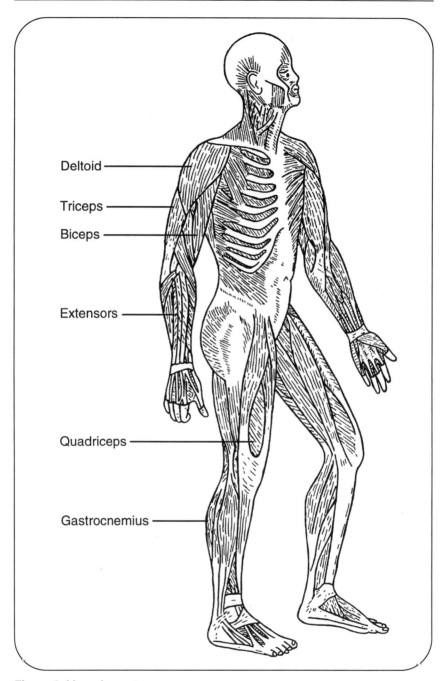

Deltoid

Triceps

Biceps

Extensors

Quadriceps

Gastrocnemius

Figure 6. Muscular system.

choose to flex or to relax them. Two other kinds of muscle—cardiac and smooth—are classified as involuntary muscles because they function automatically, outside of our conscious control. Cardiac muscle is found only in the heart. Smooth muscle exists in the arteries, the bronchioles, the digestive tract and the uterus. Spiritual power correlates principally with skeletal muscle, since it produces movement of the limbs and maintains the posture of the body. Cardiac and smooth muscles are parts of organs whose primary functions correlate with other spiritual qualities.

Difficulties with the power characteristic may manifest as disorders of the skeletal muscles and the limbs. One common symptom is tension in the muscles of the neck and shoulders. Tension in or overuse of any skeletal muscle may cause myofascitis (inflammation and tenderness of the muscles and of the fascia or fibrous tissue that surrounds them). When this occurs in back muscles, one may have a backache. Power blockages also may cause muscle cramps; pulled or strained muscles; bursitis (inflammation of a bursa, which is a fluid-filled sac that eases movement); tendonitis (inflammation of the tendons); arthritis (inflammation of the joints); or injuries that damage the limbs.

To heal any disorder of the larynx, the muscles or the limbs, employ techniques from each of the three zones of power: spiritual-mental, soul-emotional and physical. Begin by speaking the word, for this has the greatest power to harmonize mind, soul and body. Then, reprogram any memories and feelings that are impeding the healing you have called forth. Physically, utilize the best of all available therapies. Via these multiple methods the one Power, Spirit, will restore your health.

COLOR VISUALIZATION
Deep Aqua

The color for power is deep aqua, similar to the turquoise stone. This is a blending of the blue of faith and will with the green of wisdom and judgment. Blue also represents the heavens, the spiritual forces above; green, the growing plants for nourishment here on the Earth planet where we express in our physical form. As above, so below. Blue is above, green is below. So, in deep aqua we have an equal balance and blending of the spiritual and the physical. Blending these two zones of activity with the pure white of divine love creates the color of deep aqua.

Also take into consideration future, present and past. As you visualize aqua being added to your life and activities in the implanting of the I Am

91

characteristics, know you are unleashing energies which affect your past memories and soul participations; your present environment, conditions, relationships; and the future roles and missions you are working towards in the full manifestation of the light body.

Wear aqua garments with great dignity, recognizing the responsibility and the attitude of power and spiritual position those on the Christ realms comfortably bear. Spread your aqua aura protectively over all you survey. Reign regally in the I Am consciousness.

SONG INSPIRATION
Power

Power, spiritual power
Flowing, keeps me going.
On and on I go, and I know
The power here inside me is much more
Than I've begun to realize.

Power, spiritual power;
One source, I'm never without it.
Muscles move my limbs; I can do
'Most anything I try.
With God to move me, I can fly.

Power, Spirit is the power
Moving, moving all around me.
I can live today and evermore.
I can leap and run and levitate.
I can speak and sing and radiate.
I know the power; Spirit is the power
Moving, moving all around me.

I can live today and evermore.
I can leap and run and levitate.
I can speak and sing and radiate.
I know the power; Spirit is the power.
I know the power; Spirit is the power.
Spirit is the power.

7. Imagination

Metaphysical Interpretation: *Nathanael Bartholomew*

Physical Data: *Thalamus*

Color Visualization: *Crystal Clear*

Song Inspiration: *Imagination*

METAPHYSICAL INTERPRETATION
Nathanael Bartholomew

The first positive, active responsibility of the I Am Self in personal individualization is to receive and to send images regarding specific and unique functioning within the entire race form of the Christ manifestation.

This imagination characteristic is not to be confused with the creating of fanciful entertainments. Spiritual use of the imagination is the ability to receive purely, impersonally and objectively those thought patterns which are constructive and productive, which feed the soul, the mind and the body. In the light-body functioning of the I Am Self, these same proper images also are sent out in a pure and impersonal manner to be made manifest in a physical, material form.

Nathanael Bartholomew, one of the twelve apostles of Jesus the Christ, is the representative example for the correct use of this faculty of imagination. Nathanael literally means *a reward from God, a gift instructed of God.* These rewards from God and instructed by God are our Elementary Spiritual Powers (ESP). Through our I Am Self they convey information and inspiration. They formulate, through our imaging process in the brain, how to bring those ideas into manifested form.

Bartholomew, the surname of Nathanael, literally means *one who is furrowed or prepared to receive the seed.* The first six characteristics— faith, strength, love, wisdom, will, and power—have completed our trinity involution as children of God into matter form; in this case, physical bodies of the Earth dimension. By implanting the first six of these divine characteristics we have furrowed or have prepared the consciousness and the light body to receive the seeds for specific roles and missions. The seeds are those ideas and purposes, projects and services which nourish us in our evolutionary explorations.

There are three remarks made by Jesus regarding Nathanael Bartholomew which give us insight about the characteristic function this apostle plays in the drama of the Christ or I Am development on Earth. Upon meeting him for the first time, Jesus demonstrated his own gift of clairvoyance by saying, "Before you came into my view, I saw you sitting under the fig tree." Of Nathanael, Jesus said to the other followers, "Behold, a man of Israel in whom there is no guile." Israel represents a group or a nation of spiritual thoughts and ideas. Nathanael, who has no guile, has no preconceived error ideas or notions, but is receptive to whatever gift or revelation God, through his individualized I Am Self, places into his crystal-clear, glasslike imaging faculty. He is waiting receptively for the seeds his I Am Self places into his already furrowed and prepared consciousness.

Because of Nathanael's receptivity and imagination, Jesus then told him (our I Am Self tells our own imagination characteristic), "You shall see heaven open and the angels of God ascending and descending upon the son of man." *You shall see* indicates the ability to recognize; even to seeing beyond the physical range, through the spiritual sense of clairvoyance. *Heaven open* means the etheric or real world of energy and beingness, no longer hidden from the mortal, clouded or veiled physical senses. *The angels of God ascending and descending* are those thoughts or agents from the etheric and the celestial planes rising into the imagination for inspiration; then descending through the imagination in order to bring the ideas into manifested form. *Upon the son of man* indicates that this imaging quality is possible through the physical form of third dimensional matter; that is, the physical apparatus we use on Earth and through which our spiritual Self projects itself on this planet for learning experiences.

Once more we return to the brain. As in the first six characteristics of the involutionary process (Son of God descending into matter), in the first of the remaining six characteristics of the evolutionary process (son of man ascending back into light-body form), that magnificent mechanism of the brain is the key. Here at the seventh step we are concerned with the thalamus, a way station or integrating center that is located just below the cerebrum in the center of the head. The thalamus correlates with the third-eye chakra in the astral body. The information impressed on the third-eye chakra via the ESP faculties is carried to the thalamus, and from here to the various regions in the cerebrum, where it is consciously experienced and anchored.

Through the Elementary Spiritual Powers (ESP) the I Am Self communicates directly with its mortal, personality self. These thoughts and images must come through clearly and without any preconceived ideas of what the mortal mind or the soul experiences have remembered. If any interference from the mortal or the soul level occurs, one is seeing the ideas of God in a distorted way—what Paul called seeing "through a glass, darkly."

The glass or mirror through which the I Am reflects into the mortal mind via the third-eye chakra and the thalamus must be clear as crystal, uncolored. These pure reflections of spiritual intent or images are to be made manifest through the other spiritual powers and faculties; through telepathic communication; through clear knowing (clairsentience), clear hearing (clairaudience); through psychometry, the clear feeling or sensing of vibrations from other forms, whether they be animate or inanimate objects.

The term *channeling* has come into use in the New Age for these various expressions of these higher, light-body talents and Elementary Spiritual Powers. On a lower evolutionary level they would manifest as psychic powers. But on the higher level of demonstrating the I Am Self they are the basic senses and faculties of the spiritual, light-body form.

Channeling of communications is only one type of spiritual talent. Another form is channeling of energies of a healing nature; not just healing the physical form, but the astral or soul body as well as the mental and the emotional bodies. These are the areas where thought forms and experiences are collected, as in the computer bank, and then externalized through the physical body.

These Elementary Spiritual Powers are an extension of the I Am Self, through the doorway of the subconscious or astral-soul body, into Earth expression via the physically manifested form. That is why the doorway has to be clear, uncluttered, without any preconceived or limiting barriers, so the spiritual images can pass through unimpeded.

Once we have completed the first six characteristics of the I Am Self, we are led to the doorway, by the characteristic of imagination, whereby the mortal or son-of-man form may be transformed into the Son-of-God, light-body form. Being a doorway or a gate, imagination also allows the personality (the unenlightened mortal man) to reach up to those proper spiritual ideas, inspirations, communications, guidance and so forth which the I Am Self is channeling down uninterruptedly. Through this door the agents of God—be they thoughts or messengers from the etheric and the celestial planes—are ascending and descending into our Earth experiences.

The imaging process or characteristic is a key to action on an individual and personal basis. Although all derives from an impersonal, omnipresent God, manifestations of It or Its creations are distinct and individual; no two are alike; there are no duplications in functions, purposes and experiences.

The imagination characteristic is the first active principle in the dual or twin partnership of the remaining six functions of the I Am Self (see chart on page 78). Nathanael Bartholomew's partner is the apostle Thomas, referred to in the Gospel of John as the Twin, who represents the characteristic of understanding. Through the characteristic of understanding we perfect the five physical senses. Without these we cannot sense, know, comprehend fully the surrounding environment and the conditions which assist or inhibit us in development for the present time and place. Imagination (through our Elementary Spiritual Powers) coupled with understanding (via our five physical senses) enable us to be in this finite world and to be in and to explore the infinite realms at the same time. We are in the world but not of it. We are using simultaneously both the physical body and the light body.

Through the twin characteristics of imagination and understanding, man has been seeding and reaping marvelous fruits to nourish the mind, the soul and the body for eons. Some have been expressed in the fields of religion, philosophy, education, creative arts, science and industry. Anyone who has been pioneer, inventor, explorer, innovator or artist has expressed in one degree or another the imaging faculty.

Ludwig van Beethoven, indisputably one of the masters of music, stated, "I do not create music. I listen and what I hear, I write down." Beethoven was deaf in his mature years, and at the time he composed the greatest of his masterpieces. Therefore, what he *heard* was not from the physical senses but through the inner, spiritual hearing beyond the Earth vibrational frequencies. In his way he was channeling music of the spheres.

Once man comes to recognize his spiritual, eternal origin as a child of God and begins to use consciously the twelve divine characteristics inherent in his spiritual nature, the mystery and the struggle to produce these creative fruits will be gone. With an open, uncluttered door to the imaging characteristic, each person will be free to bring into manifestation those special, unique, individual fruits of his own.

But we must remember that these gifts or fruits of God through the individual I Am Self are not given for their own sakes. They are fruits produced from furrowed minds, ones which are plowed and willing to accept whatever seeds are planted there by God. Whenever there is misuse or abuse, wherever the individual tries to promote a selfish purpose, the fruit has blemishes, distortions, imperfections.

Therefore, in the developing of all these gifts—be they for art, philosophy, government, science, or mystical and religious teachings—

the purity and the perfection of the seed or the gift must be planted in a clear and uncluttered mind-field. It matters not what type of creative expression is brought forth, so long as the instrument is impersonal, loves all equally, and seeks to contribute unselfishly to all of mankind. These are the qualifications of the I Am Self in action. Anything less brings forth only partial truth.

The history of the race is replete with these impure hybrids. Most who are renowned in all the fields of creative expression are unaware of the spiritual aspects of their contributions, or how they produced their great fruits. In only a few cases throughout the history of man on Earth do we attach the honored title of master, for few truly are geniuses. In such instances invariably the individual has some recognition of the cosmic principles and energies involved in his or her works.

Increasingly in the New Age there will be educational materials to help those with these natural gifts to channel them from the I Am Self via the imagination and the understanding characteristics. But art forms are not the only fields through which creative talents are expressed. They are only one aspect of the I Am Self's creative abilities.

At this point we must realize that we receive most frequently and clearly impulses and inspirations from those areas in which we have experience. The recordings in the astral body, to be externalized through the third-eye chakra and the thalamus, can more easily dispense information already programed. This data includes experiences and information from past lives and episodes of this incarnation and from those on other dimensions, planes and planets of which we have personal knowledge and relationships.

Thus, some of the major fruits of a channel, an artist, an inventor and so forth may be in the area of that person's soul experiences. The impulses to which the person responds, either from his memory bank or from elsewhere via the third-eye chakra and the thalamus, then would be within a range acceptable and familiar.

Take as an example the three children of Fatima, Portugal, who from 1915 to 1917 had a series of nine visitations from a messenger they called an angel and from a lady they identified as Mary, the mother of Jesus. Lucia dos Santos, age ten at the first incident, saw the visions; the next year, she both saw and heard; the last year, she saw, heard and conversed with Mary six times. Francisco Marto, who was nine, saw the messenger and the lady speak, but never heard what they said. His sister Jacinta, age seven, saw and heard the messenger, but only saw the lady the first time, then both heard and saw her five more times. Yet, in all of the church and the medical investigations, the descriptions and the information from each of the three were similar, if not identical.

These examples illustrate that although a manifestation of a higher frequency range occurs, only certain of the ESP faculties may be cognizant of it, according to the conditionings, the experiences or the training of each individual. Diverse perception is common even for physical events, such as in the case of accidents, where each person remembers or responds to different stimuli.

The same is true during group meditations. Teachers, guides, masters or celestial beings send forth complex information from the higher frequencies. One person may feel a change in body frequency. Another receives a mental impression or message which answers a specific and personal question or problem. A third sees colors or auras, lights or visions. Sometimes a highly developed and experienced channel in the group can interpret the various facets received by the others and draw a single inference or conclusion from their divergent experiences, and thus create one sensible form or composite picture from the various individual and unique parts.

According to the clarity and the variety of experiences projected from one's soul memory are the extent and the strength of images impressed upon the conscious mind. The imaging characteristic is the doorway through which the higher vibrations enter and are translated through the individual, the group, the society, the environmental structure, the nation, the planet itself.

The light body of the I Am Self always is there. It is eternal and never detached from its created form, the personal self in incarnation. It, or agents cooperating with it, constantly are sending signals, information, guidance, assistance and so forth for whatever is needed. In a manner only consistent with each individual's self-preparation, receptivity, desires, openness to receive can those images, inspirations and information accomplish the purpose of gradual evolution and spiritual development.

The memory bank responds according to the needs and the records of the individual. That is why there are no two responses alike. Each one is special and unique. In part this also explains why there are prodigies and geniuses. They are responding to past training, a great deal of prior effort and interest; perhaps lifetimes of application in certain directions.

According to how much data is recorded in the computer bank, that is how each creative fruit or production is brought forth, easily or with difficulty, is considered new or trite, becomes an innovation or a repetition. However, this does not mean that those who have developed certain talents and are familiar with certain fields of expression automatically respond to the same patterns in each new embodiment.

When new and higher evolutionary thought forms are sent out, through the higher planes down into the Earth's frequency, they can be received by those who are receptive to or experienced in that level of consciousness. But just because they are sent out does not mean they automatically are picked up and rebroadcast by those capable of this. For, as Jesus mentioned in one of his parables, there are some seeds which fall upon rocks and never take root, others which fall among thorns and are choked off, while still others fall along the path and are eaten by birds. But there also are the fertile mind-fields, furrowed like Bartholomew, in which spiritual seeds take root.

What does this mean? By the various conditions of the mind and the soul do the seeds of Spirit flourish. Therefore, through all ages have the wise sages advised: polish your souls; cleanse the mirror of your being so you may reflect clearly the divine images projected to you. When we understand more specifically how our imaging faculty works we may apply it successfully and may demonstrate it.

The soul is the gateway or the door through which the superconscious, I Am Self expresses into the physical via the mortal self. The basic Elementary Spiritual Powers are those higher senses used on all planes and dimensions, regardless of which frequency or materialized form one needs as a vehicle through which to express. The soul thus is the mirror or the crystal reflecting past, present and future images. Keeping this mirror polished (removing marks, scratches and distortions) permits the I Am Self to impress clearly the images and the thought patterns on it, and thus into the conscious mind. Actually, there is no separation. There only is a reflection by the Self through the mirror of the soul out into the physical expression and form.

This is a two-way mirror. If the soul or the mirror is clean and clear, that which is outside the mortal self on the Earth level reflects into the soul without interference or blockage. Correspondingly, that which the personality self experiences from within is impressed onto the soul mirror clearly, without any clutter or distortion.

We attract to ourselves those experiences, persons and circumstances we are ready and are willing to experience (our high Self decides and controls what is introduced for our evolutionary progress). We reflect into our soul mirror to the degree we are willing, able and cleansed enough to recognize. In other words, through the aid of our five physical senses (understanding) we record information about this temporal world; through our Elementary Spiritual Powers (imagination) we receive information about the soul's past responses to similar circumstances, and also additional I Am guidance. The two acting in harmony (Nathanael/ imagination as positive-active principle with Thomas/understanding as negative-receptive principle) provide the total data about any new condition or individual with whom we are required to have new experiences and thoughts.

Grasping and utilizing this cosmic principle at the seventh step of imagination are extremely important, because the first three pairs of dual characteristics (the involutionary aspects) are reflecting down into the mortal personality, mind, soul and body. To the extent we comprehend and put into active practice this principle, we evolve the personality self back into light-body manifestation.

As above, so below. Visualize the triangle pointing downward as flipping over and up into the triangle pointing upward. Downward is the I Am reflecting into the mortal, physical self: involution. Upward is the mortal self, through the imagination characteristic and faculty, lifting itself to the I Am expression: evolution.

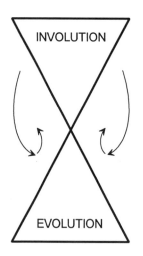

Only by seeking the higher will and special design from our I Am Self for the particular incarnation, purpose and mission in the present moment of now may we receive and carry out those images (thoughts, inspirations, plans, instructions and guidance) which are being sent into our body form, mind and personality that have been prepared to receive them. If our mirror is prepared, polished, cleansed, without damage, it receives and resonates perfectly to the vibrations and the thought patterns channeled into it. If there are distortions and imperfections we have neglected and not removed, they will be included in what our mortal self will express.

The spiritual images from the higher Self and from those on the etheric and the celestial planes are impressed on the auric field approximately two feet from the physical body. Consciously or unconsciously,

102

those who are receptive—such as channels, prophets, seers, artists, inventors, those meditating and seeking inspiration—extend their receptive senses approximately two feet from the physical body. Because of the many series of experiences in this and past lifetimes, this can be an automatic reflex action when one thinks, meditates or is receptive to higher guidance. Thus, few are even aware they are doing this. But the new images are put into the auric field first. So, whether or not the channel knows of this, he intuits or spiritually senses the new idea or image. The image registers on the third-eye screen and then is broadcast to the thalamus, which in turn conveys it to the cerebrum.

It might be worth investigating the thalamus when certain aberrations of the mind are diagnosed; for example, in those cases where persons see or hear information which has not been induced physically, or where sudden psychic openings occur as a result of a blow to the head. These conditions often are uncontrolled and undesired by the person so afflicted. Possibly they may be traced to problems in the thalamus. Perhaps such research would aid many in institutions who are being treated for illusions or hallucinations, but are instead the victims of an organic brain disorder.*

But the thalamus is not where the image, the idea or the inspiration appears. It appears in the third-eye chakra of the astral body. The third eye receives signals from the I Am Self or from others, then transfers them to the thalamus. According to the past experiences of the individual, those signals are sent to the portions of the brain which receive input from the five senses. The cerebral centers respond with sound, vision, thoughts, feelings, smells, even taste sensations sometimes.

Some metaphysicians say that imaging takes place within the mind. For instance, image that five loaves and two fishes manifest enough food to feed a crowd of five thousand people. Do this within your consciousness; envision it in the forehead region. However, this is only part of what actually is happening. The image or the picture we visualize really is projected via the thalamus (operating as a movie projector) onto the astral screen about two feet from the physical body. There it is focused. Depending on how much spiritual energy we transmit into that pattern or image, that is how closely the manifestation resembles the primary idea

---

* Current medical research on the effect that altered brain chemistry may have on the thalamus is beginning to show promise. Note that I received this impression about thalamic dysfunction in 1975. See "Physical Data" section.

and how quickly it comes into materialized form. Of course, there are other factors involved also in materialization.

The same is true in the sending of spiritual ideas or images. The higher in consciousness we have been and are striving to become, the higher our frequency radiation and thought patterns; the more lasting, more effective, more beneficial they can be. So, in creating visualizations or imaging ideas and desires for new patterns and experiences, our success depends on how much practice we have in this lifetime and in other lives, how clear and perfect our concepts of cosmic laws and principles are, and how pure and unselfish are our motives.

Jesus said, "The Father and I are one." This easily could be the theme of the imagination characteristic for the I Am, light-body functioning. What the Father or the Creator is, so is the child. There can never be a separation of these two, for they are of the same nature and substance. What the Father or I Am desires or projects out, the child responds to and must echo.

Jesus also said, "Those who see the Father, see the son. Those who seek the Father, find the son." He meant that those who truly are seeing and seeking divine will and truth may see them reflected through the son's actions and teachings. But he also meant that each individual seeking to do the will of the I Am Self (the Father within) would have to do right in speech, thought and action on the physical level. The son or the I Am images the needs for the mortal, personality self. Being one with the I Am, our Father, we respond accordingly to those images.

Remember, never in his teachings did Jesus say that the Father is the same as the son or that the physical manifestation is the same as the light body. They are two parts of one whole. They have to act in unison as one. But the higher Self is the divine being, and its created image and likeness are the mortal, personality self, a reflection of the I Am Self. At lesser stages of evolvement and comprehension of spiritual laws, this duality is quite difficult to understand and to act out in perfect, harmonious, natural ways. But in the higher, more evolved state—particularly at this stage of birthing the light body through the present Earth vibrational frequency in the Mark Age period and program—it becomes quite simple, clear and obvious. The time has arrived for these demonstrations, and nothing can hold them back from manifesting now.

Before the ending of this transitional age of marks there shall be one hundred and forty-four thousand light workers who will demonstrate the twelve divine characteristics Jesus the Christ set forth in that lifetime, through the Christ teachings, to his apostles. Let us explore the potential of this imaging quality as it will be expressed before we leave the Mark Age period and program and enter fully into the Age of Aquarius.

All manifestation concerning the involution of the I Am into personalized individualization and, from that material form, evolving back to the original spiritual expression of the I Am Self passes through the auric field. This is the doorway of the soul. These images in the astral body are carried to the physical via the thalamus. Therefore, to create a desired image or manifestation, one must first image and manipulate it through the auric field.

For instance, a master on the level of Jesus is able to see the auric field and the problem or the distortion in it which causes the difficulty in another's body, mind or soul. Being able to intune to the divine, I Am pattern of the person and having at his command the Christ characteristics and powers, he implants, changes, manipulates or corrects the auric field according to the proper purpose. Through his Elementary Spiritual Powers and by calling upon pure etheric energy, without distortion or prejudice or judgments of a mortal nature, he purifies and adjusts the other person's auric field.

All of this can take place in an instant, just about as long as it takes for the conditions to be received via ESP impressions. Then, according to the need of the person being healed and the experiences of the one in the I Am state of mind, the latter may translate the energies from the third eye in a number of ways: a vocal command, a soul reading of the person's past history (this life or others before), a telepathic message or spiritual instruction, a clear vision.

Jesus again provided our examples. By a vocal command he ordered lower astral entities to leave those whom they were possessing. He read the soul history of the Samaritan woman at the well. He instructed the lepers on their past sins and what methods they must use to complete their healings. In a clear vision he saw Nathanael sitting under the fig tree, ripe and ready for the appearance of the anticipated Messiah. Each of these is an example of the Christ Self impressing the mortal (Jesus) with specific and individual needs for others; then pressing out into the other person's auric field those desired conditions to bring about wholeness or healing, repentance or balance; and remanipulating and reimaging the error states which that person had created by misapplications of spiritual energies.

If the mortal expression, such as Jesus in this case, already has the faith, the strength, the divine will and the spiritual love, the power and the command over all the lower forces of being, then the healing of the condition may take place within several moments; or what the unenlightened and uninformed in the ways of spiritual science refer to as a miracle. But regardless of whether the change takes a moment, a day, weeks or years, even lifetimes, the process of revisualizing and manipulating the images into the auric field is a matter of the healer's spiritual development and powers, plus the level of receptivity and the karmic conditions of the recipient.

In the Age of Aquarius the citizens of the I Am Nation will have to carry this understanding of imaging to a still higher evolutionary step for groups, societies, religious movements, scientific developments, nations and so forth. According to how much error, selfishness, ignorance, fear and the like that the various individuals in those groupings have poured out, that is the amount of cleansing and healing needed. According to how much truth, love, power, spiritual energy that two or more can muster in concerted action through a balanced positive-negative force field, that is the ease with which the changes may be made manifest in those groups.

First, the new image for change should come from within the grouping or the congregation itself. Second, it must be beyond the present level of expression: more spiritual, more impersonal, less selfish and profiteering than is prevalent in the masses. Mainly, the proper image has to be held, regardless of negation and resistance to its active force and its intentions to reverse the status quo.

Return again to our prime example, Jesus of Nazareth. Although the Jews had based their religion and society on the truth teachings of Abraham through Moses, David and Solomon until Jesus' lifetime, and although they believed strongly that they were the people chosen to represent the concept of one God, they still had incorporated into their national system many distortions, evils, errors and pride. But the conditions then were no different than those which are so prevalent in our society, theologies or governmental systems of the present day.

Jesus' major function, and also the prophecies regarding the coming of the Messiah, involved the reimaging of those error patterns. He came to raise the force field of those congregations to a higher spiritual level of service and functioning for the planet. That meant rooting out and defining what the errors were. Then he demonstrated and taught reimaging of the new and higher concepts and practices; first for the I Am Self of each one, then for concerted action by congregations of spiritually enlightened persons for the nation.

The Master had twelve major apostles; the twelfth later was replaced because of corruption beyond reparation at that time and in that place. He had hundreds of disciples who followed and obeyed him. In addition there were thousands from many nations, backgrounds, affiliations, heritages and religious convictions who listened, considered, contemplated, waited for proof, thought about and tried to follow his thinking and examples.

Likewise, each of us has twelve apostles/characteristics which we too must reform and bring to new levels of understanding and functioning. And if that should mean that we must rehabilitate one of our characteristics because it betrays our real intention and purpose to become Christed, we must have the courage to do that totally and without hesitation. We have thousands of thoughts, experiences, preconceived ideas and images which must be converted to a higher level, according to truth and spiritual standards, in order for our entire being and all the cells of our body to operate cooperatively and harmoniously as an individual I Am nation or Self.

We must begin to extend our thought processes from individual I Am Selves to the whole planet and the entire race of man on it. The cosmic principle involved is: what affects a single cell of the organism (a single soul in the body of mankind) affects the whole; also, what affects the whole affects each of its parts. Therefore, what affects each soul in the race of man here affects the race itself, the planet, all life forms on the planet, all the astral beings who have been or in the future will become part of the Earth experiment. Those souls who express from the I Am level of consciousness know, from the thought patterns and the images impressed upon their soul computer records (that portion of the brain which remembers all information), that the ideas and the information they radiate from this region affect all life forms and elements within the environment of which they are but a single part.

Stability for the dawning Age of Aquarius also is involved. For as the changes and the transmutations take place, those on the I Am level of consciousness are fully aware that there are within the whole group those who can accept these changes slowly or at a medium rate or quickly, and others who may react with total rejection, even turning and rending the new. Although the reimaging process is an inherent Son-of-God characteristic and a natural spiritual power, the master consciousnesses cannot personally be responsible for the reactions to the need for reformation, rehabilitation, change and transmutation.

Each one has his I Am to guide and to process these changes in a harmonious manner. But the master of spiritual energies and characteristics knows the magnitude and the potential inherent within his reimaging powers, and holds steady to the proper course and desire in spite of the variables due to the free will of those involved. This same principle applies whether it involves our personal thought patterns or those congregations of thoughts which form groups and societies.

Jesus set many examples for us. He was aware that his work and demonstrations might take an age—two thousand years, at the most—to become fully manifested for the race, the planet, and all forms and species on it. In fact, he told his apostles that it possibly would be at the end of the Piscean Age and the beginning of the Aquarian Age before he could return and claim the spiritual kingdom of which he was teaching them and proclaiming himself Prince. None of them really understood this then. Many followers afterwards have expected him to complete these demonstrations in their lifetimes.

But, as mentioned already, the ability to translate the information from the master level of consciousness to the mortal self of others is possible only to the levels of their acceptance and understanding. So, although the imaging faculty of the master is clear and uncluttered, when he passes the data into the spiritual senses of the recipients it may become distorted or be blocked there.

Distortion and blockage account for the varied levels of understanding and application of spiritual students. For instance, the apostle Peter's functions, comprehension and mission to be accomplished could be quite different than those of other apostles. Jesus replied to these differences by saying in effect: "What has his responsibility or job got to do with you? You do what I have asked you to do. Don't be concerned with what I have given to the others. Just follow me."

We each must respond individually to our own high Self instructions and purposes. We must try to express fully what our I Am has commissioned us to complete. Our concern cannot be about another's progress or specialized function, or even possible errors. By focusing on our own missions and responsibilities we have inevitably a direct effect upon the whole group. First we change ourselves, specifically and individually. Then, in united action, we may serve the whole nation of I Am beings and bring forth successfully the I Am Nation on Earth.

Our planetary work as a race of beings in the light body is coming to a climax in this Mark Age, known as the harvest time or Latter Days. Jesus set the pattern, gave the examples, issued the prophecies concerning our work, individually and collectively, for imaging the coming Age of Aquarius and for planning and implanting the I Am Nation.

Our bodies, our levels of consciousness, our talents, our relationships are the total of what we have imaged for ourselves and have worked on in retribution, restitution, repentance and have recorded in the ledger of life, have earned for good or for bad. According to our individual, and later our collective, abilities to comprehend the past, the present, and to some degree the needs for the future, we can reimage the necessary changes into the auric patterns of ourselves and the astral envelope around the Earth planet. We see, by knowing and sensing the right conditions, the information compiled in the computer parts of our brains. Then, as a result of these implanted new images, each one and the race as a single body respond to those images emotionally; in ideas, inspirations, plans; and finally by actions.

This is not to imply that all we think, feel, say and perform must be expressed physically. Many things are computed through this system that do not materialize in outer, physical forms. There are images, ideas and thought patterns projected into our astral-subconscious aspects. They may not solidify into an outer manifestation until another life expression; or they may manifest in more subtle ways, such as through character structure or personality, emotional developments and tendencies, or philosophical ideals.

All that we experience through thought and word or deed is impressed on the auric field and becomes part of our soul records. To change that, we have to work through this same doorway or auric field of the soul body.

Therefore, if we image and desire things from the mortal, selfish, psychic, emotional levels of our expression, we receive composites on those frequency levels, for that is what we have programed into our computer records. However, if we have cleansed the mirror or the image mechanism, our soul records, then the images impressed into the auric field are clean and clear from the I Am Self. Then, according to the faith, the strength, the love, the wisdom, the will and the power which we previously have developed and implanted, we translate the new images quickly or slowly, strongly or weakly.

The purer our motives, the clearer the image. The more unselfish our desires, the longer we can maintain the image. The more we gain in new talents, the greater our services, the higher our functions, the happier we will be. Conversely, if our views are selfish and limited, if our mortal ego interferes with the clear and pure vision from the I Am Self and its infinite potential, then we experience pain, distortion, unhappiness, difficulties, severe tests and trials in our evolutionary growth.

Jesus admonished us, "Do not resist an evildoer." *Evildoers*, or enemies, refer to thoughts, plans, conditions, acts, persons who would not allow us to function fully as the I Am beings we truly are. They also could refer to diseases, poverty, family relations, friends, business associates, the society or the government in which we are participating. Do not resist negative conditions there by returning still another negative condition. Do not fight these enemies.

Instead, if we accept the cosmic law of cause and effect—that we reap what we have sown, somewhere, sometime, for some reason—we must recognize that we implanted the relationships or the conditions of our present experiences, and they are pressing outwardly into our present circumstances. The higher spiritual law teaches us that in such unsatisfactory conditions we must start re-forming in our auric field those corrective images that are Spirit's desire and need for us now. Always Spirit's desires and needs are for our highest advantage and learning and discipline; in general, our greatest good and our highest potential.

Following Spirit's will for us by reimaging—which is our divine heritage and one of our twelve spiritual characteristics—we rehabilitate, recondition, reset relationships and conditions in our lives. It does not mean we have to like what we go through in the process, or have to like the conditions requiring regeneration. Nothing in the cosmic law says we have to love these enemies as they are expressing, even if we have contributed to their creation. What we must love is the spiritual faculty our all-merciful Parent has given to us; and that is our ability to rehabilitate, to re-form, to reimage all according to the perfect pattern God desires for His-Her children.

It doesn't matter if this perfect pattern takes years, lifetimes, even ages, to re-create, as long as we remember we are reassembling these energies *properly*; meaning, according to the proper balances and spiritual laws, which favor not one above the other, which consider all conditions and persons equally for each one's highest good and potential. According to each one's level and experiences with the reimaging talents, that is how fast, how fully, how well the new images supersede the old ones and dissolve them. This is how we conquer our enemies.

Spirit through our I Am Selves is the force and the energy and the pattern by which all is done perfectly. Man, in the evolutionary process, using his co-creative powers as a child of God, is relearning these techniques and characteristics of the divine Self in order to live, to produce, to experience in that eternal I Am consciousness.

For example, disease is an enemy. In most cases, it appears in our auric field or in our thought patterns before manifesting in the outer, physical form. Reflecting on such a condition, through the imagination quality we are capable of remembering past actions and thoughts which permitted that pattern to develop first in our auric field, then to reflect from there into our brain computer, finally to be broadcast or to be printed from that recorded data into a form of physical or mental aberration. Whatever form it takes, we always get exactly what we deserve; or, to put it technically, the printout is exactly according to the data we personally programed into our computer.

So, instead of resisting this enemy, hating it, planning revenge against it and thus compounding error thought patterns, we must learn to read the data about this pattern. Next, we seek to determine what caused it to be present. Was it karma earned from a past life? Was it a series of thoughts and philosophies we learned from our society, family, associates in school or business? How did we pervert the spiritual laws into man-made interpretations and methods?

Denying the error patterns exist, resisting them, or fighting back on their level only reinforces and strengthens them. Allow them to be eaten and destroyed in the auric field by the higher vibrations of spiritual concepts and laws. The I Am Self constantly projects cosmic truths and remedies for these mortal creations through the third-eye region and the soul-auric field. Open up to these fearlessly and honestly, without preconceived ideas and plans. The third eye is the mirror which will reflect the perfect form, personality and life experiences on the present dimension of expression.

We may have to repeat the reimaging process often. But once we recognize the system as the purpose and the means of the I Am Self, timing becomes less important. Unfailingly and without faltering, we must apply faith and strength, perseverance and understanding.

PHYSICAL DATA
Thalamus

The thalamus is an ovoid or egg-shaped structure that is located in the center of the head, below the cerebrum and above the hypothalamus. (See Figure 7.) Actually, there are two thalami, each of which lies beneath one of the two cerebral hemispheres. The two thalami are joined together on their middle surface.

The thalamus serves as a relay and integrating station. Information gathered by the five physical senses, except smell, travels via sensory nerves to specific thalamic centers, which relay it to specific sensory centers in the cerebrum. For example, visual images received by the eye are transformed into nerve impulses that travel via the optic nerve to the lateral geniculate body in the thalamus, which transfers them to the visual center in the occipital lobe at the rear of the cerebrum.

The thalamus also serves as a relay or way station for the ESP faculties or psychic senses. Intuitive, psychic impressions register first in the third-eye chakra in the astral body. They anchor into the physical body at the thalamus. The thalamus relays these images, ideas, symbols and feelings to the cerebral centers wherein the psychic input is perceived, analyzed and understood.

The nerve connections between the thalamus and the cerebrum are reciprocal. New images created via the mind and the cerebral circuitry trigger nerve impulses that travel from the cerebral centers to the thalamus, which then projects the image into the auric field at the third-eye chakra. At the same time, the thalamus relays the nerve impulses it has received to the hypothalamus and the medulla oblongata. The hypothalamus controls pituitary hormonal secretions, which regulate other endocrine glands and numerous body functions. The hypothalamus and the medulla also send signals, via sympathetic and parasympathetic nerves, to regulate the activities of every part of the body. Via these pathways, what we envision becomes a physical reality.

Difficulties at mental, emotional and soul-astral levels with the spiritual quality of imagination may cause imbalances in the thalamus. However, due to its location deep in the center of the head, and because it secretes no hormones or other substances into the blood which can be measured, few medical tests currently diagnose thalamic disorders. Newer brain-scanning techniques (including CT, MRI and PET scans)

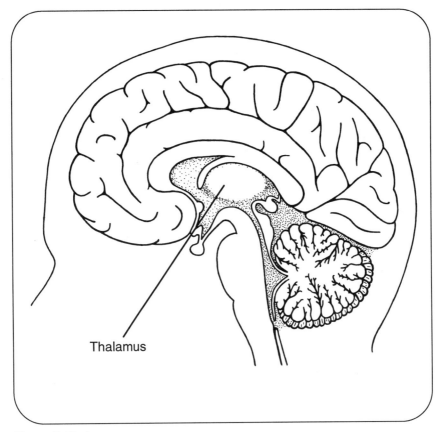

Figure 7. Thalamus.

do provide pictures of all parts of the brain. Nonetheless, even these advanced technologies have yet to delineate common thalamic imbalances. The only thalamic disease listed in medical texts is death of thalamic tissue caused by a stroke that blocks blood flow to this organ.

Researchers have postulated that an imbalance in the thalamus may cause hallucinations. The thalamus is thought to serve as a gate or a valve that determines the amount of sensory information that flows through it to the cerebrum. Neurotransmitters regulate this valvular function. (Neurotransmitters are molecules that may enhance or inhibit the transmission of nerve impulses from one neuron to another.) When neurotransmitter levels and functions in the thalamus are altered, the valve opens wider and allows greater amounts of sensory input to flow through it, causing a sensory overload in the cerebrum which may lead to hallucinations. One way brain chemistry is altered is by ingestion of hallucinogens such as psilocybin (found in some mushrooms) and lysergic acid diethylamide (LSD), which are similar in molecular structure to the neurotransmitter serotonin. However, use of hallucinogens is definitely not recommended.

Since common medical tests currently do not diagnose thalamic disorders, other means must be used to determine if the imagination quality and the thalamus are functioning in a balanced, harmonious way. Pressure or pain in the forehead, extending at times to the temples, may indicate difficulty with the imagination faculty. Imbalances may be revealed in dreams, in which the third eye and the psychic senses are symbolized as a window, a doorway, a hallway, a tunnel, a clear crystal, a mirror, a television screen, or a single, all-seeing eye. In dreams, meditations or moments of clairsentience, or by consulting with a competent psychic, one may recall past lifetimes in which one demonstrated the psychic talents either in a masterful or a distorted fashion. Review of the present life may indicate that some intuitive impressions were received clearly, whereas other inspirations and visualizations were colored by mortal desires.

Whenever you discover imbalances in the imagination characteristic and the thalamus, follow Jesus' advice to keep your eye single. In other words, via your third-eye imagination faculty visualize wholeness, harmony, balance and health. What you see, will be. Your mind, soul and body will be filled with light.

COLOR VISUALIZATION
Crystal Clear

Crystal, mirrorlike glass, any neutral transparency may be related to the characteristic of imagination. These are the elements upon which we may build or reflect something else. They do not radiate images of their own; they must reflect whatever is projected into them. Therefore, reflect something desirable, wonderful, good, positive, constructive, happy and beautiful.

One useful metaphor is Lewis Carroll's fictional Alice in *Through the Looking Glass*. Alice stepped into the looking glass of her imagination and entered into a wonderland of experiences. Alice is the mortal personality of the present time and place. The mirror is the soul and the imaging characteristic of the spiritual Self.

114

Create characters or individuals, circumstances and societies, expressions and experiences which are desired by your Christ Self. These are representative of the higher inspirations and teachings of the etheric and the celestial mastership planes. See all of these coming to life, breathing and moving about. Watch the drama reflecting into this mirror of the mind and soul. Step into that image, and live and interact with it.

Remember, you have created everything in your life this way. So, if there is something you don't like in your life, health, thoughts, relationships, now you have the method whereby you can re-create it. Through your imaging faculty, your Christ imagination, life is what you see it to be.

SONG INSPIRATION
Imagination

I've got this gift, imagination.
I envision the world being whole.
I give this gift, imagination;
I give it to the world to make it whole.
I make new images of light to heal the planet.
I make new images of light to heal my soul.
I use new images of light to see before me;
I imagine what the future's going to hold.
Imagine people of all races free and strong,
Joining hands and never, never knowing wrong.
I imagine there's a place for me to be
In this picture of the future that I see.

I create as I use imagination;
I set new patterns into motion all day long.
I hear clearly, I see clearly,
I know truly what is true.
I'm prepared to let the light of God
In me come shining through.
I make new images of light to heal the planet.
I make new images of light to heal my soul.
I give this gift, imagination;
I give it to the world to make it whole.

8. Understanding

Metaphysical Interpretation: *Thomas*

Physical Data: *Five Physical Senses*

Color Visualization: *Cream Yellow to Pale Orange*

Song Inspiration: *Understanding*

METAPHYSICAL INTERPRETATION
Thomas

Of all the other characteristics which are paired in a dual, positive-negative polarity, those of imagination (Nathanael Bartholomew) and understanding–illumination (Thomas, called Didymus) are the most inseparable. Both the given name Thomas and the surname Didymus mean *twin, twain, joined, conjoined.*

The physical functioning or counterpart activity for the spiritual person is that of the five physical senses—seeing, hearing, smelling, tasting and touching—along with the rational and analytical aspects of the conscious mind. Working inseparably together, these create an image or a picture of the world in which we function on this Earth plane or third dimensional frequency.

It is not just that man has greater development of the five physical senses than the other living creatures on this planet. But the race of man has joined them together, in conjunction with his ability to rationalize and to analyze conditions, to allow him a unique position and a more composite, true recognition of so-called physical realities and situations. In order to survive in their natural environment, some animals have evolved greater ranges and sensitivities in one or more of the physical senses. But no physical organism has evolved a more complex, integrated, harmoniously balanced use of the five physical senses with the rational and analytical mind than has the race of man. Our senses are in pairs also: two eyes; two ears; two nostrils; taste receptors on both sides of the tongue; and touch receptors on both sides of the body.

Thomas, in his representation as apostle for the five physical senses, is the most misunderstood of all the twelve divine functions; just as the five physical senses are the most misunderstood by those seeking to become spiritualized and to express in the light body. We have coined the term *doubting Thomas* as ridicule or disappointment. We have come to consider it less than devoted or evolved or spiritually oriented because Thomas, as the physical sensor and rationalist, asks for proof on the mundane level. He would not have been an apostle of Jesus the Christ if he had doubted the higher realms, the inner plane functioning, the beyond-the-physical-frequency events, or so-called miracles.

The physical senses of the body and the conscious, rational mind or reasoning faculties do not deny the supersensory I Am functions and abilities. But while the physical body and the conscious mind are extensions of the I Am, they also must have evidence that what is being claimed by the other senses, functions and characteristics actually is being performed or is operating. The physical senses report to the brain computer and the limited, mortal expression or personality self what is occurring here on the three-dimensional, five-sensual world. The higher, more subtle ranges of ESP (psychic senses) report to us what they pick up from the invisible vibratory levels.

When Jesus said to Thomas, "Blessed are you in believing what you can see [hear, feel and so forth], but more blessed are those who can believe without seeing," he was not condemning the function, or asking it to atrophy or to be eliminated from the physical. Our I Am Self tells us that we are more blessed and rewarded when we can believe in the workings of our spiritual Self without requiring physical proof. But physical proof is necessary and desirable in this present physical world. The two realms, physical and spiritual, must work in harmonious, joint cooperation.

As long as there is an outer, physical extension to the inner, invisible spiritual cause, it is essential that there be means of verifying and experiencing both realms simultaneously. This joint, inseparable, twin functioning of imagination and understanding gives us the comprehension of balanced functioning and becomes true illumination; the soul with the spirit, the mind with the body, the physical self with the I Am Self.

Every realm, every situation, every function, every responsibility has inherent limitations. Without comprehending those natural fences or borders, we constantly would be and are overstepping the bounds of right action and the proper use of our tools and instructions.

Spirit does not infringe on the gift of free will for Its creations; although, since It gave free will to begin with, it appears that Spirit would have that right. No master infringes on the development, the choices, the rate of growth of his disciples; otherwise, he forces a premature development, which can be more damaging and limiting in the long run. In nature, the parents do not force the chick out of its shell, but let it gain strength by pecking its own way out. These analogies indicate that the strength of the physical form or the personality structure—with a good reasoning, intellectual mind which can examine all conditions surrounding all events—serves the individual on the physical in the environment where that individual must function as a counterpart of the spiritual Self.

The five senses and the questioning rational mind are the tools which convey to the individual those limitations within the environment or those conditions in which he is temporarily and mortally bound for a time. It is ridiculous to say, as would some spiritual students, that there are no physical limitations and requirements in this three-dimensional, five-sensual world of mortal existence. Jesus certainly demonstrated that the mortal part of man is subject to mortal conditions. But the spiritual man, the I Am Self functioning in the light body, overcomes those limitations and boundaries.

Of course, everything must be put into its proper perspective. It would be equally wrong or ridiculous to separate physical from spiritual; or to say spiritual conditions happen only in spiritual realms and physical things only may be experienced in and are limited to the physical Earth level. That is why Thomas, called Didymus—representing the five physical senses as they report to the reasonable, rational, mortal aspect of mind—is doubly named *the Twin*. The two are in harmonious oneness, operating simultaneously and for the common good of the whole being: spiritual man in a physical form.

The agonizing cry of humanity, generally speaking, is: we don't understand. Understanding is the key to love, compassion, faith, will; in fact, to all the other eleven divine characteristics. This is further proof that each of the divine functions serves each other one. All are inseparable, interdependent, purposeful needs and tools for the whole being, the I Am Self.

How do we come to understand anything about life, about other people, about other creations and species, about life in other realms and planets, about abstract ideas, new inventions or concepts? By and through the evidence of our five physical senses and their counterparts on the inner planes of living, those senses we call the Elementary Spiritual Powers, do we perceive and understand.

There are none so blind as those who will not see. Sages throughout time have said: those who have ears to hear will hear what I am saying; those who have eyes to see will understand what I am doing. These aphorisms really mean that only understanding reveals truth. But the key to understanding any realm, inner or outer, is through the senses indigenous to that realm.

The ability to understand why a condition, good or bad, is manifesting as it is on the inner or on the outer realms comes from putting together all the facts contributing to that condition. The operation may be likened to that of a computer, which must access all pertinent data and programing in order to produce a valid readout. Likewise, to reach true understanding, the conscious, reasoning, analytical mind must access all physical as well as spiritual factors that contribute to the condition.

Apply this analogy to any situation (planetary or local), any condition (mental, physical or soul level), any person (living or dead) you personally do not understand fully. Do you know all physical and nonphysical factors involved in creating that, as it appears to you and at the level of your present understanding? Are there factors—most certainly there will be—you have not had revealed to your conscious mind (computer)?

Not until all the factors are put into the computer bank—and that takes all the readings from all the senses, both physical and spiritual—can you truly get a definitive, comprehensive, reasonable readout on that person, condition or situation which eludes your comprehension. There is nothing to say that when you do get all the facts you will like the person, condition or situation any better. But you certainly will know how to deal with it more reasonably and effectively, because you will have more information and details at your disposal.

Spiritual man does not work with partial facts, be they ESP data or strictly physical information. The I Am slowly and deliberately, through understanding all factors involved on all realms connected, takes action in proportion to mental, physical, emotional and soul needs and abilities to receive whatever action is appropriate in thought, word and deeds, or any combination thereof. When the light or the truth of many statistics comes into consciousness, these enlightening factors illuminate the mind and present an understanding which serves the entire being and many diverse functionings of the Self.

These statistics do not always come through the physical senses. They are presented to the conscious, analytical, reasoning mind from past memory banks and from higher guidance through the I Am Self and the guides and the guardians of higher planes who are cooperating with and assisting all of us simultaneously in order to express the higher aspects of our being.

Jesus, the I Am representative, understood the key role of this divine characteristic. Perhaps this is why at the Last Supper he washed the feet of his disciples, saying that if he did not do this for them they could not serve properly him and one another. To metaphysicians, feet often symbolize the understanding nature, because it is upon the feet that we stand on Earth, and the feet hold up the entire vehicle in which we operate. That part of us which touches and connects with the Earth plane matters must be cleansed of all dirt and debris which interfere with spiritual understanding.

Examine how understanding and illumination serve all the other apostles/functions of the I Am Self. Without understanding the facts of limited situations on Earth and the methods of operation on the higher planes of existence, faith is blind and wavering, sinking beneath the waves of turmoil. With understanding, faith is firm as a rock and as unshakable. Without understanding and proper illumination, the strength is strictly willpower and is forced. Without understanding, love, no matter how sincere and desirous of service, has no depth or direction. It is nice to feel love, and for others to know you feel it, but what can love do without understanding?

There is no wisdom or proper judgment in any situation without understanding the facts that contribute to it. Expressing divine will without understanding why and what you are doing in that situation makes you as a puppet without a mind of your own. The use of power and mastery without understanding and considering all the factors over which you have command is senseless and can be ruthless. The faculty of imagination in setting forth proper images into the ethers for manifestation, without understanding the environment, the consequences, the efforts involved, the basic history of the past as a foundation upon which to build the new and desired image, simply is fantasy; is not based on fact, truth or reality.

To develop and to direct an organization or to put a system of operation into effect without understanding the needs, the future potential and the capacity of each part of the organism is chaos. To express zeal or enthusiasm for a job or a function without understanding the facts involved burns out the purpose before it can become a lasting and beneficial flame, a light or a beacon in the darkness of our efforts. To call forth a regeneration of the life force within, to reproduce more of the same of our thoughts, lives and creations without understanding their place and service in the future, is to bring forth more things or conditions than we can control or can use productively in the situation where we are operating at present.

Lastly, to deny what is, to try to eliminate what exists without understanding the principles and the necessities of that renunciation essentially is to throw the good out with the error. There is no discrimination, judgment, sorting or grading of the information and the needs involved in the situation.

Understanding, like all the other faculties and apostles, serves each one of the others and the whole Self. By going through the list even superficially one by one, we realize understanding and illumination hardly can be limited to just the five physical senses as they compute into the data bank of the rational, reasoning part of the conscious mind. Understanding and illumination must come from: (1) many past episodes of the soul; (2) many new inspirations which the higher Self implants during the time of need or exploration in the new areas of experience; (3) the wisdom, the guidance, the new factors which those of higher consciousness present to illuminate further the individual.

Those of a higher consciousness acting as mentors or guides may be on the same plane of operation—teachers and leaders with whom we are in personal contact. Or they may be leaders in fields we only have heard or have read about, who stimulate the mind into new areas of thought. All we hear about or consider—as well as all we personally experience and physically do—goes into our computer bank. From other planes of existence our guides and guardians also impress ideas. In a sense, leaders of other fields of endeavor in the entire race of man—either on the visible planes of life or on the ones invisible to our conscious awareness—stimulate us, force us to stretch our understanding beyond the status quo.

Take for example the man-into-space programs since the 1960s. The majority of Earth citizens are not involved personally in developing this scientific research or in experiencing the flights. But the efforts of a very small percentage of the human race in this exploration have broadened all of us in our understanding about our bodies, minds, technology, future place in the solar system, use of certain products and other helpful items in our daily lives. We all are changed by the understanding of certain factors and experiences imposed upon us by a very small and highly specialized minority of men and women.

This same principle applies to those who are doing creative, innovative, breakthrough work on the inner, spiritual planes of existence: hierarchal program workers, mystics, prophets, inventors, explorers and so forth. Their understanding and efforts impinge upon the subtle regions of the brains of the rest of mankind. We pick up this information as thought patterns. Eventually the new concepts and data become incorporated into our conscious thinking, rational minds to be dealt with in analyzing certain conditions and in making certain decisions.

The same applies to those working on other planes and planets who are radiating out, and possibly imaging into our auric force fields, the new facts involved in our present society and evolutionary patterns on Earth. Our brains, like sensitive radar devices, pick up this information or guidance. By our very nature we must compute it along with all the other data in order to achieve broader understanding and greater illumination of ourselves, one another, the planet and all the universe.

With this approach to understanding, we also recognize why some individuals understand more, more quickly, more easily than others. Depending on the receptivity, the lack of blockages, the past experiences of similar data, certain ones can absorb or can compute the information and can use it to gain understanding of the present condition they need to deal with. It is not so much that some are superior to others, for we all have the same equipment. All are receiving, more or less and in one way or another, the same input from the data processor, the brain computer. But in some individuals the analyzing section is freer, more experienced, less cluttered in comprehending the incoming information.

For instance, here is an analogy that is used frequently to teach the evolution of spiritual consciousness. It is the one concerning the relationship of the caterpillar to the butterfly. Suppose a butterfly were able to explain to a crawling caterpillar what it is like to fly, and tried to describe all the beauty, exhilaration and freedom of flight to the limited, uninitiated, unimaginative and earthbound worm. Might not the short-sightedness of this caterpillar lead him to disagree with the butterfly, even to the extent of thinking he is mad? There is nothing in the caterpillar's experience to allow him to relate to the expansions and the potentialities the other relates. But the butterfly, who already has experienced the metamorphosis from caterpillar into cocoon into butterfly, has the knowledge and the experience personally that this is the inevitable evolutionary process. Someday that same caterpillar may try to explain to another caterpillar what it is like to be a butterfly.

All of us have been exposed to people with very conservative, limited, hard-shelled, blind-by-choice points of view. Such individuals refuse to consider any condition beyond the ones they personally have experienced, or that are outside the teachings of some religion, nation, political conviction, occupation and so forth. This is not to say, either, that every person is crystallized and limited, like the caterpillar in our parable, and is bound to resist instructions offered by one who already has experienced the full cycle of metamorphosis. There are some who, through prior memory and instinct and by utilizing the five physical senses and the analytical process, can anticipate and can project themselves into other areas of experience.

Another example more pertinent to mankind is the differences of development and functioning of the species in the two sexes, male and female. Many men cannot comprehend the functions, the needs, the conditionings, the limited physical opportunities of females in their society. In this example we take into consideration that sociological and geographical conditions greatly influence the opportunities and the accepted activities of each of the sexes. So, a Muslim shepherd from a small Arabian village certainly would not be able to understand the thinking, the actions, the desires of a woman executive in an advertising firm in New York City. But he would be capable of understanding and computing all the factors if someone applied time and effort to presenting all the information about our fictional woman, and thereby gave him the prerogative to analyze her actions and her desires for expression in her own environment and with her particular set of responsibilities and functions.

The same lack of appreciation, understanding and illumination applies to our modern woman, in regard to our primitive man; since, even with her advanced knowledge and book learning, she would not have to use the same senses and aptitudes in her existence as does the shepherd in his desert, nomadic lifestyle.

The spiritual faculty of understanding and illumination becomes one of the most important and constantly changing and evolving aspects of our higher Self in action wherever we are placed. For if we accept that life on Earth in any one experience or incarnation is merely a temporary and short episode in the long history of soul evolvement, then understanding and illumination grow from out of the past into many present experiences and lead into multitudinous opportunities for the future. Understanding and illumination feed the other faculties of our spiritual Self and force our mortal limitations beyond present, or even near-future, goals.

No one can ever experience or know (details, data, information) about everything that exists in eternal creation in the myriad levels of experience throughout all God's kingdoms and species. Therefore, new information, new experiences, new insights constantly are being fed into the computer bank for the understanding of life and our part in living as children of and co-creators with God.

126

A word of caution is required here. Because the function of under-standing must be applied with all the other eleven functions or character-istics of the I Am Self, those who feel especially drawn to this aspect might overapply and overemphasize its role. One could intellectualize too much and become bogged down in myriads of data and information. One also could say: I don't have all the facts and figures, therefore I can-not make a decision; I don't fully understand everything that is involved in this situation or condition or the other person's behavior.

We never will learn all there is to know about almost anything. We never will know everything that has occurred everywhere. Therefore, we have to temper this extreme devotion to understanding and illumination with wisdom, faith, love, and the need for organization and system in carrying forth a particular mission at a particular time in a particular place.

There are none of the faculties or the parts of the divine Self being developed here on Earth for birthing the light body which cannot be overstimulated, overused, abused and misused. All aspects must work in conjunction, harmony and balance with, and in respect for, each of the others.

PHYSICAL DATA
Five Physical Senses

The spiritual quality of understanding–illumination corresponds to the five physical senses and the reasoning, analytical aspect of the con-scious mind. The eyes, the ears, the touch receptors, the taste buds and the nose convert different third dimensional stimuli or vibrations into nerve impulses that travel to specific sensory centers in the cerebrum. Not until the sensory nerve impulses reach the cerebral centers are they perceived and interpreted as images, sounds, touch sensations, tastes and smells. The logical, reasoning aspect of the conscious mind functions primarily in and through centers in the left cerebral hemisphere.

Vision. The eye's cornea and lens bend light passing through them and focus it on the light-sensitive retina at the back of the eyeball. (See Figure 8a.) The retina contains rods and cones. Rods are sensitive to light intensity, providing vision in dim light. Cones detect color and fine detail. Rods and cones transform the colors, forms and images they re-ceive into nerve impulses that travel via the optic nerve to the thalamus,

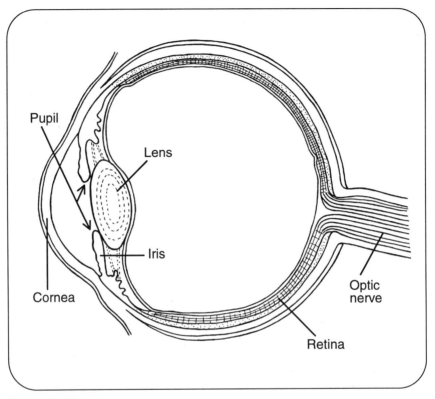

Figure 8a. Eye.

which relays them to the cerebrum's visual center. Visual input accounts for about eighty percent of our sensory awareness of the physical world.

Hearing. Sound waves are funneled from the outer ear through the external ear canal to the tympanic membrane (eardrum), making it vibrate. (See Figure 8b.) In the middle ear, these vibrations are transferred via three bones—the hammer, the anvil and the stirrup—to the oval window of the inner ear. The vibrating oval window causes waves in the fluid in the cochlea; the waves in turn move hair cells in different parts of the cochlea, thereby triggering nerve impulses. These impulses pass along the auditory nerve to the thalamus, which sends them to the cerebral hearing center where they are interpreted as sounds.

The inner ear also contains the labyrinth, which is used for balance. It contains three semicircular canals at right angles to one another. Head movements cause fluid inside the canals to move, which creates nerve

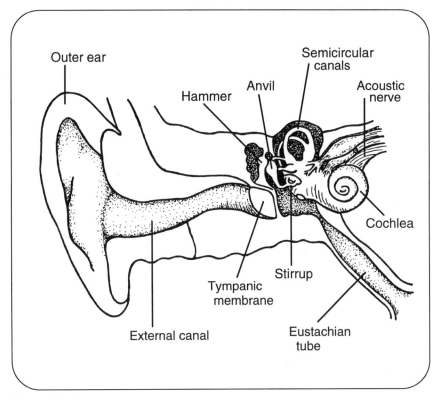

Figure 8b. Ear.

impulses that travel to the thalamus and then to the cerebrum. From this input, the cerebrum determines the position and any movement of the head. This data is coordinated with sensory information from the eyes and the body's muscles to determine what movements the body must make to maintain its balance.

Touch. The sense of touch includes many subdivisions: light touch, crude touch, pressure, vibration, pain, temperature, two-point discrimination, and proprioception. Each of these has a specific receptor organ that converts the touch sensation into nerve signals, which travel via sensory nerves to the thalamus and then to the touch center in the cerebrum.

Taste & Smell. The tongue's taste buds respond to four major tastes—sweet, salt, bitter and sour—which trigger nerve signals that travel to the thalamus and then to the cerebral taste center. However, ninety-five percent of the ability to taste relies on the ability to smell.

Volatile substances release molecules that stimulate the endings of the olfactory nerve in the roof of the nose. This initiates nerve impulses that travel via the olfactory nerve directly to the cerebrum's smell center.

Mental, emotional and soul-astral difficulties with the spiritual quality of understanding may cause or contribute to disorders of the five senses. Eye disorders include nearsightedness, farsightedness, astigmatism, conjunctivitis, corneal infections, iritis, retinal detachment, cataracts, glaucoma, and eye tumors. Ear disorders include outer, middle and inner ear infections; Ménière's disease and labyrinthitis, which cause problems with balance and vertigo; and partial or total hearing loss. There may be alteration, diminution or loss of taste or smell, or of one of the aspects of touch. Problems with understanding also may cause difficulties with conscious reasoning, as in learning disorders (such as dyslexia) and mental imbalances (including severe ones such as psychosis).

COLOR VISUALIZATION
Cream Yellow to Pale Orange

Dwell for a moment on the desire to improve any one of the five physical senses, or on the ability to reason and to analyze any problem, with the intention of using the corresponding color(s) upon those areas in yourself.

The average response will be: please do not apply anything sharp, strong, harsh or powerful. For all the physical senses are extremely delicate instruments and require a fine balance. Too much pressure, too much attention, too sudden an adjustment can be painful and disturbing. The very nature of our senses is gentle balance and delicate tuning. Too much light, extreme darkness, high and low pitches, loudness and softness, strong odors, imbalanced chemicals in food or drink, pleasure or pain via touch, and so forth upset the equilibrium immediately.

In the same respect, concentration on the conscious, reasoning aspect of our thinking apparatus usually requires the utmost diplomacy and consideration. Otherwise, turmoil and confusion result immediately.

Therefore, the colors to be applied in meditation for implanting corrective and desirable vibratory rates to the physical senses require special consideration and gentleness. Cream yellow is almost a white, with only the slightest suggestion of mental activity and stimulation. Pale orange suggests a complementary determination, devotion; with strict discipline that does not imply severity.

Because the senses and the reasoning nature of our minds fluctuate so quickly and with the slightest and most subtle of variations, it is necessary to allow these delicate shades, from cream yellow to pale orange, to play freely and unrestricted upon the screen of our visualizations.

SONG INSPIRATION
Understanding

Understanding is the marriage of the heart and of the mind,
Of that source of inner wisdom and the things our senses
  find.
Listen to that still small voice within; let understanding
  grow
Like the gradual unfoldment of the petals of the rose.

chorus
I understand, I understand
That there's more to life than the senses sense
And the brain can comprehend.
I understand, I understand
That life takes on new meaning
When I seek that source within.

Lift the dark veils of confusion from my troubled mortal
  mind;
Let me see those many visions that the spirit shares inside.
Let my ears always be opened to those innermost vibrations.
Let me grow in the understanding that can awake the
  sleeping nations.

chorus
I understand, I understand
That there's more to life than the senses sense
And the brain can comprehend.
I understand, I understand
That life takes on new meaning
When I seek that source within.

131

9. Order

Metaphysical Interpretation: *James son of Alphaeus*

Physical Data: *Digestive System, Skeletal System & Skin*

Color Visualization: *Mustard Yellow*

Song Inspiration: *Order*

METAPHYSICAL INTERPRETATION
James son of Alphaeus

Just as we often refer to God as love, the purpose behind all being and creation, so we as frequently speak of God as law and order. One of the greatest wonders in all creation is recognizing the systematic, orderly organization in all things. In both the greater and the lesser creations we are awed by the interrelating interdependency of all working together harmoniously and rhythmically. From the strictly intellectual approach, the magnificence of such precision, orderliness and intelligent management baffles the reasoning mind.

In examining even the most miniscule, seemingly insignificant creations, still we find simple and orderly systems operating. Therefore, if the smallest of elements and creations function in this orderliness, how much more so must the race of man, who is called the child of God and a co-creator with Him-Her, function similarly?

Both through the I Am, light body and the mortal externalization or physical framework of the I Am Self, man must function in an orderly and systematic way. It is the responsibility and an unconditional requirement of the spiritualized mortal being to know about, and to respect and to work cooperatively with, the mechanism through which the individualized I Am Self functions.

James son of Alphaeus, whom scholars often refer to as James the Less, enacts for us this characteristic of our Christ being. His appellation as the Less (or the younger) is to differentiate between him and James son of Zebedee, who represents wisdom, justice and judgment in our twelve divine characteristics. There is no coincidence in having two named James, for James signifies *discernment and judgment.*

In James son of Zebedee, the wisdom and judgment attributes are used for the purpose of guiding the endocrine system in order that it distribute properly all the spiritual energies from the I Am, light body throughout its externalized physical form, our Earth body.

In James the Less, who is the son of Alphaeus—which name literally means *leader, chief, organizer*—the lower functions of our Earth body require a manager to keep the physical form operating within a framework suitable to the conditions, the environment, the vibrations where it is incarnated, in order that the I Am Self may perform its immediate duties and fulfill its destined mission on Earth.

Again we refer to the symbol of the Star of David; six pairs of two triune principles, equaling twelve divine characteristics (see Figure A on page 9). They represent first the trinity of the God Self involuting into matter, and secondly the trinity of the child of God descended into materialized form and evolving back into I Am expression. So it is that James son of Zebedee judges and manages our light-body functions; and James the Less, son of Alphaeus, judges, manages, organizes our Earth-body functions. As in the Star of David symbol, all twelve qualities are equal to one another; interdependent, interlocking, and each one serving the other eleven.

James son of Alphaeus is the organizer, leader, distributor of physical substance throughout the body temple of the son of man. So, he symbolizes the digestive system, which converts and distributes substance from all the elements in our environment for the nourishment and the continuation of that form. Likewise, this apostle represents the skeletal framework through which our bodies can perform, plus the skin, which provides us with a protective covering over all our other organs. Without an organized framework and an outer shield to protect it, there is no system or order, nor any possibility for continuity.

It requires tremendous discernment and wisdom of the I Am Self to keep the body temple, the house through which it functions in this limited environment and dimension, working in a harmonious, healthy, organized way. For we are required not only to perform physical functions through this framework or body temple but to develop and to learn and to experience soul lessons.

Since our soul functions require as much, if not more, vital substance and energy as our physical ones, we need managers and organizers for both light-body performance and physical-body duties. Scientists, both of spiritual and physical laws, recognize that considerable energy and substance are expended through mental and spiritual activities. Psychic sensitives realize that during certain periods of productive and concentrated meditations, healings, communications and such, more of the physical body's reserves are burned up than if the same amount of time were devoted to physical labor.

Therefore, any manager of a factory—which, in a sense, the physical body temple is—must make wise and discerning decisions about the distribution of the natural energy supply throughout the complex system, if it is to remain productive, balanced, healthy, harmonious and, above all, running smoothly without interruptions.

Examine here this analogy of the factory to our body temple. The building, the facilities, the purposes of manufacturing are limited. The factory is not intended to be infinite, nor does it have infinite resources. Likewise, our individual incarnations and physical-body expressions are limited, mortal frameworks for a specific function and purpose of our infinite I Am Selves. Each incarnation of the I Am Self has a special purpose, job, function, responsibility and time allotment.

Each is allowed just so many resources in the way of funds, supply, storage, machinery and laborers to carry out the job for which it was created. Any factory/personality assuming too much responsibility, or trying to perform the function for which another was created, overloads and confuses the system. Any expressing apathy or lying down on the job causes wide dissatisfaction through the system, worry, idleness, and eventual deterioration of the entire operation.

One single aspect within each person, as well as only one overall manager in the factory, must schedule the priorities, determine the right order for the total manufacture of the item for which the factory/personality is responsible, plan for the traffic and the shipment of those goods, if there is to be any profit gained in operating at all. Those who are specialists and are assigned to operate the equipment in the factory cannot be burdened with other responsibilities. Most times they have little concept of the general, overall needs within the complex factory/personality. Each division or system within the body/factory requires concentration and specialization. But to keep the mechanism properly meshed and integrated, a good manager or organizer is essential.

On the other hand, the manager of this factory/body cannot be expected to do the jobs for which the other laborers have been hired, nor to develop the craft necessary to perform each specialized job. Rather, it is up to the conductor or chief to set the standards, the schedules, the methods of communication from one system to the other, and to be responsible for transporting the substance or the energy to each department at the right time. The conductor is concerned with the entire operation.

Extend these cosmic systems to still another degree. It is the I Am Self who manages and controls all the varied aspects of the individual incarnations of the soul throughout all the dimensions and the systems of the universe in order to perform a specific function and purpose within the whole body of the Christ, the child aspect of Father-Mother God Trinity. It is not the mortal personality of the individual who may determine what the I Am Self is to manufacture for the whole Christ body.

137

Yet, many beginners make this mistake and do attempt to dictate to their I Am individualization what they personally want to express.

The master of spiritual consciousness should dwell on the twelve divine characteristics as twelve different departmental supervisors, responsible for the twelve different systems and functions of the physical body. Each must perform its individual, specific, specialized function. The I Am Self must demand that each system deliver to the best of its ability, according to its design and purpose. The I Am Self, as well as most who are in the mortal level, totally trusts the system works and allows it to function without conscious dictation.

In a miniature sense, our mortal bodies follow the hierarchal system of evolution and growth. We have an unconscious faith that the cells/workers in our physical bodies are performing normally, naturally, unhesitatingly, uncomplainingly. But when there is a breakdown or an interruption, the master—which is the I Am Self—should and must be able to direct the proper corrections. The remedy depends principally on the cause of the problem, whether it stems from physical, emotional, psychic or soul areas.

Generally our mortal selves are enthusiastic about affirming cosmic principles which lead us up the ladder in our ascent toward cosmic consciousness. But the mortal has a tendency not to appreciate fully the necessary balancing factor of denial. The breaking-down of the elements we ingest is absolutely essential to digest and to assimilate them properly. Both affirmation and denial are equally important to cosmic balance: plus–minus, in–out, yin–yang, build–destroy, birth–death.

Digestion, assimilation, structure and protection are as important to the spiritual Self as the discovery and the partaking of divine laws and truths. As an example, we may need and eat a whole head of lettuce because it has natural properties and elements which are beneficial to our physical-body cells. But the lettuce leaves themselves do not build into our blood, cells, tissues, bones and so forth in the same form we have ingested. Various functionings of our bodies are assigned to breaking down the fibers, refining the minerals, digesting the nourishing qualities, and still others are responsible for discarding whatever refuse remains.

Similarly, in all our experiences, thoughts, ideas, avenues of individual expression the I Am Self must break down whatever activities are participated in by the I Am in the higher frequencies, the mortal self in the Earth plane and the soul on the astral levels. It is one of the twelve divine functions of the I Am Self to sift the wheat from the chaff of our experiences, to eliminate the tares and the thorns of our associations, to distribute those good and constructive ideas into the soul record for the future planning and developing of new, evolutionary and productive projects.

Eventually the time will come, in an orderly and progressive step, to be unmerciful in discarding whatever rubbish clings to the experiences or the associations to which our flesh is heir. There are parts in many plants which really can harm, which can clog the system if eaten, which need to be torn off or eliminated. There is no shame in elimination. It is part of the natural, orderly, sensible—wise, really—cosmic system of things.

Time and patience are important in this divine system. Experience immeasurably aids in discernment. Too much, especially in Western cultures, does man look at speed as some special attribute of progress and accomplishment. Orderly organization, proper digestion of all elements, then fair distribution throughout the system cannot be judged solely according to the speed by which the job is accomplished.

Returning to the factory analogy, assembly-line production in a modern automobile factory is no substitute for a custom-made, individually designed, unique and personalized vehicle. The retort that many cars are produced in the same time as one special, highly crafted auto in no way satisfies the higher requirements for quality, safety, long-lasting use and extreme value.

The evolving master consciousness is trying to build spiritualized cells and ideas to last indefinitely. Speed and duplication are of no consequence in this consideration. Transmutation from the physical, mortal, three-dimensional frequency form into the spiritual, eternal, four-dimensional light-body functioning is slow and gradual because it is for permanent and lasting results in use throughout the universe. It is not limited for strictly temporary operations on this planet and for just this one life span.

In the reprograming and birth of the light body through the mortal vehicle, we must work methodically, deliberately, slowly if necessary, cell by cell. Accept the fact that we have been at this evolutionary process for twenty-six million years as a race on Earth, ever since man fell into materialized-matter form in order to experience this third dimensional frequency. Our gradual uphill climb is not meant to be by spurts and starts, sudden and quick. Purposely it must be deliberate, gradual, infused with commonsense judgment and understanding.

Eventually we must transmute one hundred and forty-four thousand centers in the central computer, the brain. It is from the main organ, the brain computer, that all the cells of our body/factory, all our past ideas and memory-recall information, must change from the dense and dull vibration of physical, third dimensional frequency into those of a spiritual, fourth dimensional vibration. This transmutation takes time and patience, deliberate planning and management.

Those who feel the need for miracles, for sudden and swift changes in themselves and the world around them, who are troubled by the progress of the hierarchal program externalizing on Earth now, should examine closely their own lives for proper organization and systems. They should try to discern if they correctly and fairly have judged and have digested all the information concerning past, present and future developments of the race as a whole, as individual segments within the race now expressing on Earth, and especially their own personal contribution to the race evolution.

There is a proper time for planting seeds, for nurturing the first shoots and then for harvesting the fruits. This is the systematic and orderly process for every type of manifestation, even for those that are abstract, such as new inspirations, plans and philosophies. Proper spiritual development and growth must take place in an orderly progression if the fruits of the original desire are to be ripened to the fullest and thereby give the best nourishment.

Each step in the growth pattern requires an individual, special time and a unique method in order to develop fully and well. There is no such thing as rushing or skipping the proper sequence of events. Some may fool themselves by inventing rationalizations and systems they claim cut short the growth period. But the fruits of such systems inevitably turn out to be either unpalatable or too sour or too sweet for remaining in the system very long, or they lack proper nourishment or satisfaction of any kind.

Those of us who wish to bring forth the I Am Self must organize the priorities of development in correct, sequential and practical order. There is a time to study. There is a time to meditate on what we have learned; which does not necessarily mean we are to accept everything we have studied, but rather are to sort out what is usable and is constructive to individual needs. Then there is the time to apply what we have learned.

If all these things bear fruit and actually enhance one's understanding, service, happiness and bring progress mentally, emotionally, physically and spiritually, they have proven themselves to be of good (God), at least for that individual if not for others. But if these things bear nothing productive or nourishing, then additional periods of eating, digesting, sorting, assimilating and eliminating are mandatory for the birth of the light body.

At every step along the way to Christhood there is some form of digestion, assimilation, reorganization taking place. The full realization and eternal experiencing do not occur all at once, one time or eternally. This is a continuous process, an ever-present characteristic and function required to nourish the I Am individualization. The order function provides a substantial framework through which new experiences can be formulated. Every time we learn and experience something new it is necessary to allow a period to put it into the system and to gain another perspective. The events of yesterday are food for today, and provide new cells/ideas for tomorrow's visions.

Where we as a race and as individuals came from and what we did yesterday and thousands of lifetimes ago determine the conditions for what we can accomplish and experience today. Where a person fits into the vast social spectrum, what responsibilities are presented in the present hierarchal plan on Earth, what talents have been developed and can be expressed for personal evolution and the benefit of fellow beings are the total considerations of the I Am Self, and of the masters of the Hierarchal Board who assign the I Am individualization a specialized role and mission in the overall plan and program.

Depending on how each one accepts, digests, assimilates, separates and eliminates the residue from all these ideas and conditions, that is how future responsibilities, roles and missions are determined. The present and immediate absorption of all these details determines future opportunities, functions and responsibilities assigned. Performance in the here and now determines future opportunities.

If this system or orderly organization is the method by which the mortal, intellectual world operates, how much more must it be applied in the spiritual worlds. If in preparing to become a lawyer, a scientist, a space explorer, a writer or an architect it is necessary to organize study time, to examine all priorities and interests, to evaluate financial assets in order to become a professional in one of those fields, how much more so those same considerations apply in developing and studying to be a full Christed being who expresses totally in the light body.

Intrinsic to the birthing and the unfoldment of the light body is a period of organizing, systematizing, digesting everything from past experiences and the present lifetime. That includes abilities, talents, needs, desires, services, missions and other responsibilities of the I Am Self.

Once this process has begun, ideas, memories and thought patterns from the subconscious mind begin to churn up and are dumped into the conscious reservoir. There they must be examined, analyzed, sorted, graded—the wheat separated from the chaff—with the undesirable parts permanently discarded. Though this step may be thought of as painful, it also can be a time of joy and thanksgiving. Anything done for the sake of birthing the I Am consciousness here and now is a joyous thing and is to be accepted with gratitude and appreciation.

If every event, thought, deed and plan is put into proper perspective, if every experience is examined for the good it has brought to personal development, if all error and pain are being karmically balanced, then the attitude of the I Am Self is one of awe and appreciation for God's divine laws of order, harmony, righteousness and equal justice. If this is the attitude of the I Am Self, the mortal personality is obligated to imitate it and to rise to this same level. Therefore, the inevitable period and function of order and system in examining past, present and potential future must be considered a privilege, a supreme joy, the right and the honor of God in action.

Pleasure and passion for order and organization lead directly to a sense of enthusiasm, even of zeal. In fact, zeal is the proper companion, the opposite-polarity partner, to this desire for proper order and spiritual systems operating through the mind and the life of the I Am Self on Earth. When everything in life is in order and harmony and is properly being managed, when the mind and body and soul are in rightful relationships to each other, the automatic response from the I Am level is exhilaration, enthusiasm, expectancy, hope.

The I Am Self sees clearly that the best possible period for birthing the light body at this stage of development is the sorting-out and the separating of the good from the error of all experiences, thought patterns, emotions, relationships and talents. Obviously, error thoughts and patterns, undeserving and detrimental relationships cannot exist in the Christ realms or with I Am functioning. Honestly and thoroughly we must review separations, digestion, assimilation of all that is good. Thereby we energize our primary purpose for I Am externalization, reinforce our will and determination, and nourish our resolve to be reborn into the original Christ state of consciousness.

At such times everything which seemed to be ugly or painful suddenly has new meaning and purpose. It becomes distilled in our consciousness, with only the good in those experiences remaining for building, strengthening and serving the total Self. The undesirable and the unproductive are discarded. They are replaced by right motivation, acts of discernment, spiritual judgments for the proper management of all thoughts, affairs and relationships.

All of us grow and learn not only from the good which has been in our lives but from the errors as well; that is, provided we have examined freely and have dissected thoroughly those errors, with the good parts and lessons digested and the evil parts forgiven and dismissed forever. However, if there is not true repentance of the error—turning it around fully and using it for benefits of growth and understanding—it automatically returns to the mind and to the experience through new relationships even more powerful, supported by additional allies which then create even greater mischief and havoc. This consequence, too, is part of cosmic laws and systems.

Therefore, when all this reviewing takes place in the consciousness of the evolving I Am Self there are corresponding reactions. According to how serious the review is and how the systematizing unfolds, that is how difficult and complex the physical, mental and emotional reactions can be. The mortal self inevitably responds in proportion to the higher thought activities and decisions.

Since the digestive system, the subconscious memory patterns and the psychic contacts associated with the astral realms all resonate to the solar plexus region of the physical body, it is here where symptoms may crop up. Remember, even though we are endeavoring to rise above and to eliminate past astral and lower soul-psychic contacts, nevertheless they do have an entrance area, a specific place in the auric field—the solar plexus chakra—to which they resonate and through there can enter the consciousness. The I Am Self does not deny or eliminate the functions of the subconscious mind, the feeling nature, the emotional patterns, the astral-soul body, or the physical vessel itself. They all have a place and a function in the orderly evolutionary process.

In the temporary mortal vessel the past memory patterns of soul and emotions first are absorbed through the solar plexus chakra. This region corresponds to the digestive system, which manages the orderly organization of nourishment for this plane of action.

Those who work with the lowest forms of psychic phenomena automatically activate the solar plexus. However, when one desires and invites the higher thoughts, expressions and energies, they enter through the crown center at the top of the head or the third-eye region in the forehead.

But no matter how highly evolved one is, including those of etheric and celestial realms, digestion and assimilation are part of divine functioning. Therefore, periods of sorting, examining and organizing experiences and relationships from the past, in the present and for the future, are natural and necessary.

We must consider another factor, also. Whether conscious of them or not, whether one desires them or not, each one is subjected constantly to thought developments and changes within the species or the race of which he is one part or an individual instrument. Thus there are thought patterns from the group which radiate experiences, conflicts, problems and so forth, thereby influencing each individual's development.

It doesn't matter one iota whether one is above or below average in that group's evolvement. Each one is part of the whole, and the whole affects each one of its parts. The evolutionary experiences of the entire group impinge on each one's auric field. These in turn resonate personally and specifically to the solar plexus chakra of the auric field and then affect the digestive system on the physical.

No one can escape fully the group pattern and evolutionary process, either in the timing aspect or by the particular step that is next in proper sequential order. No one can organize a life's mission and demonstration outside of what is suitable and necessary for the group development. Not even the Messiah, Christ Jesus, tried to do that. In fact, this was the very limitation or boundary he automatically responded to in many of his refusals to take overt action in the world in which he then resided, or to perform some so-called miracle in order to convince others.

Each one's personal and individualized service and mission must relate to and enhance the group's evolvement, the advancement of the race in the society or the environment where it is developing at the time.

However, there is a crude proverb which says, "If you lie down with dogs, you get up with fleas." Applied on a spiritual level, it means that those who—either by choice, karma, ignorance or experimentation—are involved more with lower thought forms, individuals or activities than are correct for their level of achievement or proper for their goals of development automatically are subject to hazards, limitations, dangers and errors inherent to those associations.

There is no point in arguing that even fleas are part of God's creations or that only from the dog's point of view are they irritating and undesirable. The point is, they represent irritants, parasites, dirt and negligence. The fleas are not in their proper place, functioning according to the best order, system and harmony of the dog. They represent something to be rid of; to eliminate after the sorting-out process, before assimilating and organizing the benefits.

The archangels have channeled that even those of the celestial realms who descend into the lower regions to assist and to serve those of lower evolvement than themselves must go through a thorough cleansing upon their return. For their auric fields pick up from the lower regions debris and undesirable particles. These produce cloggings and disturbances within their levels of operation until they are cleansed and removed.

How much more so then for man when reviewing past and present experiences, associations and thoughts. The divine system and order work on all levels, without exceptions. Examine and sort the good, the productive and the constructive experiences. Separate them from the detrimental and the destructive ones. Wisely judge each one; discerning which to keep and to digest thoroughly, then to assimilate for future advancements.

PHYSICAL DATA
Digestive System, Skeletal System & Skin

Order–organization–system correlates with the digestive system, the skeletal system, and the skin. The digestive system breaks down and assimilates the nutrients needed for maintaining present body cells and for growing new ones. The skeletal system provides the solid, internal framework for the body. The skin forms the body's external boundary.

Digestive System. This system consists of teeth, gums, salivary glands, mouth, pharynx, esophagus, stomach, small intestine (duodenum, jejunum and ileum), gallbladder, and exocrine portion of the pancreas. (See Figure 9.) Teeth cut and grind food into smaller particles, while salivary glands secrete saliva, which contains the enzyme amylase that starts the digestion of starches. Swallowing propels food into the pharynx, down the esophagus and into the stomach, which secretes

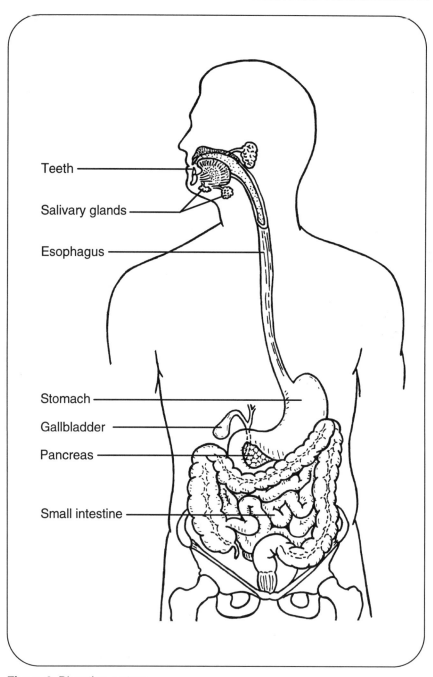

Teeth

Salivary glands

Esophagus

Stomach

Gallbladder

Pancreas

Small intestine

Figure 9. Digestive system.

hydrochloric acid and pepsin to begin the digestion of proteins.

Food next passes into the first part of the small intestine, the duodenum, which receives bile from the gallbladder and digestive enzymes from the pancreas. Bile is manufactured in the liver, and then is concentrated and stored in the gallbladder until it is released to help in the digestion of fats. Pancreatic enzymes continue the breakdown of proteins, carbohydrates and fats. The food moves next into the jejunum and the ileum of the small intestine, which release additional enzymes that complete the breakdown of the nutrients into tiny particles. These are absorbed into the bloodstream, which carries them throughout the body.

Skeletal System. This system includes bones, cartilage and ligaments. The body's two hundred and six bones are living organs composed of an organic matrix impregnated with complex mineral salts, made primarily from calcium and phosphorus, that give bones their hard structure. Cartilage is not calcified as bone is, but rather is a firm gel with a consistency similar to firm plastic. Cartilage is found in the nasal septum, the discs between vertebrae, the outer ear, the joints between ribs and breastbone, and other joints. Ligaments are tough, fibrous bands of tissue that bind bones together.

The skeletal system serves several functions. It is the body's solid framework. It encloses and protects some vital organs; for example, the skull surrounds the brain, and the spinal column encases the spinal cord. The solid structure of bones makes movement possible when muscles contract. Some bones contain red bone marrow, where red blood cells and some white blood cells are manufactured.

Skin. The body's largest organ consists of three layers: the epidermis, the dermis, and the subcutaneous tissue. The epidermis is the thin outer layer that has no blood vessels. It contains the pigment melanin, which gives skin its color. The epidermis depends on the underlying dermis for its nutrition, since the dermis is well supplied with blood vessels. The dermis consists of connective tissue, sebaceous glands, and some of the hair follicles. The dermis merges below with the subcutaneous tissue, which contains fat, sweat glands, and the remainder of the hair follicles.

Sebaceous glands secrete a protective fatty substance called sebum that keeps the hair supple and the skin soft and pliant. It also prevents excessive water evaporation through the skin. Most sweat glands open directly onto the outer surface of the skin and secrete fluid, which helps cool the body and removes small amounts of toxins.

When our thoughts, feelings and soul records are not in divine order, we may develop digestive symptoms such as nausea, vomiting, loss of or excessive appetite, indigestion, gas, heartburn or stomachache. These symptoms may accompany ulcers of the stomach or duodenum; inflammation of the esophagus, stomach, small intestine, pancreas or gallbladder; and gallbladder stones. There also may be obesity or eating disorders such as anorexia nervosa and bulimia.

Difficulty with order and organization may lead to broken bones, dislocations, ligament sprains, damaged cartilage, bruises or other injuries; with some people being "accident-prone." There may be malformed bones, bone infections or bone tumors.

If we are angry, anxious, afraid or ashamed, we may develop skin disorders such as dermatitis (eczema), psoriasis, hives, warts, boils, sebaceous cysts, impetigo, folliculitis or cellulitis.

With any of the above diseases, in addition to psychological and soul factors, always consider physical causes. If symptoms continue or are serious, see a physician and utilize the best of all remedies that medical science has to offer. At the core of your holistic treatment program, however, focus on the spiritual quality of order. Decrystallize and discard imbalanced thoughts, feelings, memories and physical practices that have caused your physical disorder. Systematically replace them with positive, constructive ideas and applications of divine order and organization. Your digestive system, skeletal system and skin will be healed.

COLOR VISUALIZATION
Mustard Yellow

Mix together brown earth, green plants, yellow sunlight. The combination is a complex activity, a synthesis of thoughts, actions and colors. It is suitable, in the visualizing of this characteristic, to take each one of the processes, with a corresponding degree of color mentioned here, then to dwell and to meditate upon it separately.

Mix them together in varying degrees. Every combination and shade will be suitable and applicable to the time and the purpose of the varied stages in your individual growth pattern. At one time you will be separating and sorting, at another you will be digesting and assimilating, or ordering certain elements in your consciousness to build or to reinforce the structure and the protection concepts more securely and firmly.

The brown is for implanting order–organization–system on the Earth level. The yellow is for the strength and the stability to carry through on the instructions and the design for your I Am mission. The green is for the substance and the nourishment which come from the various sources of your experiences and associations, from the multiple conditions with which you must live.

The conscientious organizer, as in any complex system, must juggle and balance multiple and varied situations and all aspects of the organized form simultaneously. This characteristic of the spiritual Self has many ramifications and multitudinous responsibilities.

SONG INSPIRATION
Order

Order, order in my life;
Order, I see order coming forth.
Order in my thinking, order in my heart,
Order in my body; time for me to start
Putting order in my life.

I've been taking things in so fast, it seems,
That I hardly swallow one thought
Before I get another and another.
Gotta get order in my life,
Gotta digest my daily bread,
Gotta have a system, gotta have a plan.

One foot before the other, step by step,
Taking each turn as it's taken,
Not too slow and not too fast.
Gotta have order in my life,
In my skin and in my bones,
In my job and in my home;
Gotta have a system, gotta have a plan.

Divine order I invoke to rule my days and nights,
Order making harmony in every inch of me.
Order in my life, now it's time at last;
Gonna have a system, now I've got a plan.

10. Zeal

Metaphysical Interpretation: *Simon the Cananaean*

Physical Data: *Hypothalamus & Medulla Oblongata*

Color Visualization: *Rosy Pink*

Song Inspiration: *Zeal*

METAPHYSICAL INTERPRETATION
Simon the Cananaean

After all the substance and the energy for the highest good of the birthing of the light body have been distilled, and as this nourishment flows through mind and body and soul, a new level of exhilaration begins to develop. A zeal never realized before begins to manifest. Proper order, organization and system of mind, body and soul are inseparable from zeal. For when everything fits together consciously, the most natural automatic reaction is one of great appreciation, thanksgiving, joy and love. A passion to share these realizations begins to grow.

But here is a caution. Elimination has not taken place yet. For in the distillation process we only have separated, have sorted and have graded those experiences and ideas into their rightful places. Only after we thoroughly have digested all the good and have distributed it throughout the system can we demonstrate the proper zeal.

A certain amount of time also is required for the error thoughts and the negative experiences, ingested along with the good, to be transmuted and eventually destroyed or eliminated. The residue from some of these imperfections still resides in the mind, the soul and the body. Elimination becomes the last act of the I Am in birthing the light body, just as it is the final step in the physical system.

Zeal actually is an automatic and natural result from properly knowing, feeling and using all the preceding divine characteristics. We cannot force it consciously if we are to enact it spiritually. And we never should deliberately suppress it, from some false modesty or lack of understanding its purposes.

At this particular stage in birthing the light body, two distinctly different types emerge. The first comprises those who are blasé. They take for granted that they are children of God. They assume the attitude that cosmic laws exist for them as inherent rights and privileges. So, without any enthusiasm and appreciation, they automatically use the laws and treat them casually. They accept for the moment whatever experiences come into their lives, without any conscious attempt to control or to change them. The second type is made up of those who lack caution and discretion. Into their newfound knowledge they try to involve everyone and everything all at once, without any sense of discernment and discrimination. More about these two types later.

153

As mentioned, zeal is the automatic and natural sequential step after its partner, order (digestion and assimilation). First, the order characteristic must be fully activated. A separation or sorting (digestion) must be under way between those things of benefit and those others which may deter, harm or actually destroy the spiritual purpose. Simultaneously, good is being transformed into nourishing substance for the mind, the body and the soul (assimilation), so there is a holy (whole) vessel with which the I Am Self may merge.

During this process, we have examined all affairs, experiences and persons in the present incarnation. Our subconscious storehouse has brought to our conscious, analytical mind those events from the past which also need analyzing, examining, sorting and final decision-making. Our soul record has been revealed, and we have accepted, worked upon and balanced karma, both good and bad, to the best of our abilities in the time and the place where we are functioning. If we cannot pay all debts here and now in the present incarnation, we project out consciously to the high Self a desire to pay them later.

Via the characteristic of order–organization–system, we have put all things in their proper places and have accepted the proper times for their manifestation. As a direct result joy, satisfaction, peace, enthusiasm and zeal come bubbling to the surface. All is in divine order.

If this stage is not reached after we have called into service all the preceding characteristics, then our lack of spiritual application causes a reevaluation period. This may take the form of repeating the past in order to take care of any errors we could not resolve otherwise. Re-evaluation can take place in many ways on many levels, including a return to the astral for reassignment at another time and for another place.

During our regrouping and reevaluation, everything is presented again for ordering, organizing, systematizing. A different set of values or conditions is presented which may be more palatable or acceptable to us. This is arrived at through the higher guidance of our I Am Self and those masters and teachers who are assigned to our soul evolvement.

The lessons we could not digest and the errors we did not permit a time for elimination remain in our soul memory bank, the astral-soul body. From this composite new personalities are designed, new opportunities are presented, new relationships are developed. According to our individual abilities, willingness, spiritual discernment and acceptance, that is how many of the error conditions which previously hampered further soul growth are allowed to be dealt with in the next series of opportunities, lifetimes, explorations or expeditions.

The residue of the errors may manifest in various body problems, relationship difficulties, serious obstacles in the society or the groups with which we are involved. None of us is an island. We do not live alone in any world, here on Earth or elsewhere. We are associated with and connected to some form of family life, religious concepts, national or political conditions, sociological patterns or environmental limitations. Any or all of these may serve to reveal some block or clog in the soul which we must examine, sort and eventually place into the proper orderly pattern. Now or later we must deal with the soul impaction in order to evolve to a more satisfactory state of being. Everything in the experience, of course, is based on our inevitable destiny to become one with the I Am Self and to bring forth the light body.

At the point in evolution where zeal does enter and we use it properly with spiritual understanding and discernment, we are ready and willing to share enthusiastically all that is good, no matter the situation or the conditions, and we deeply desire to discard all that is unproductive and detrimental to the digestive and assimilative process.

In the wonderful drama of Jesus the Christ, the characteristic of zeal and enthusiasm is portrayed by the apostle Simon the Cananaean, appropriately called the Zealot. The literal translation of Simon is *hearing, obeying, hearkening, reported*; of Canaan, *lowland, material existence, subconsciousness, humbleness and receptivity*. In his *Metaphysical Bible Dictionary*, Charles Fillmore writes that Canaan "represents the unlimited elemental forces. . . . To mystics it is the name of the invisible substance that surrounds and interpenetrates all forms, of which it is the mother."

Within the spiritual expression of man, zeal and enthusiasm are direct, automatic responses to all the past inputs, thoughts, emotional patterns, experiences, trials and triumphs, even soul records. In the physical body of mankind there is a corresponding area at the base of the brain, comprised of the hypothalamus, the medulla oblongata, and the reticular activating system. In accord with the subconscious memory storehouse, this area at the base of the brain triggers automatic reflex actions in various physical functions of the body, such as heart rate, blood pressure, breathing rate, body temperature, water balance, desire for food, and the sleep-wake cycle.

Whenever anything disturbs these physical functions, a signal is received at the base of the brain, which in turn sends out the corrective measures to compensate for the disturbance. For example, if an emergency or an accident occurs, the subconscious past-memory center receives the message. According to past performances and patterns, an automatic response goes out, supplying the corresponding amount of energy and substance to those parts of the mind, the body or the emotions that may be required to solve or to serve the total being in that problem situation.

Does not zeal, or the lack of it, function in the same way? More than any of the other characteristics, zeal–enthusiasm is the servant of all the other eleven qualities. From this aspect we receive the impulses, the desires and the substantive needs the other characteristics require. Zeal serves each of the others with just the proper amount of spiritual energy, fervor and excitement each one requires to perform its tasks.

As we develop and reprogram this I Am Self characteristic, changes occur in the automatic timings of those functions over which this section of the physical body has control. The new spiritual programs alter the automatic, subconscious memory bank. Those who regularly engage in meditation exercises, study a special spiritual course, seek evolvement into cosmic consciousness are familiar with some of the following symptoms in their physical organisms. Different people have different responses. Sometimes these reactions occur only one time. For others they may occur frequently or on a regular basis. Each one is an individual.

Temperature Changes. Hot flashes and cold chills. Goose bumps. Internal heat, even to the point of perspiring abnormally.

Heart Rhythms. The beats are faster or slower. In some advanced states of *samadhi* (cosmic consciousness), yogi masters can control the rhythms consciously, even to the point where they appear to have no heartbeat at all or appear to be dead.

Cosmic Sounds. These may be heard inside the head, or may seem to be coming from outside of the person. Remember, this characteristic/ body function is Simon, meaning *to hear clearly the call of the Christ.* Both Simon, later called Peter, and Simon the Cananaean, the Zealot, automatically heard and responded to the call of the I Am Self. This is the mystical call to obey and to follow the I Am. Break down the code of *Simon*: I Am Son. I Am One. One's I Am. As in Om (*Om,* the holy name and sound of God).

Many hear their names called. This is a signal from the I Am Self to pay more attention to spiritual events in the life. Others hear the chiming of bells or a high-frequency buzz. More attention should be paid to these phenomena because they may result from the memory bank automatically responding to similar episodes to which the soul had been awakened in other situations.

Memory Recall. Patterns or experiences from the past life or other lifetimes on other planes and planets spring from this memory storehouse, also. Therefore, if in meditation or dream or self-analysis, thoughts arise concerning past lives and experiences they are stimulated from out of this subconscious storehouse to help and to serve all the other spiritual characteristics in order to explain or to interpret the present purposes and problems of this life.

Enthusiasm and zeal can come only after we have put everything into divine order and after we have distilled all the good from past experiences. So, it is to be expected, in our evolving to the I Am Self, that memories from the subconscious are recalled, seemed to be relived, are awakened once more into the conscious mind for rechanneling and reprograming according to higher laws and principles.

This subconscious functioning, controlling the astral-soul memories along with automatic reflex responses of the physical body, easily explains why certain failures and limitations are expressed in the physical body's performances. The past memories and patterns set up a preconditioned reflex of automatic rhythms and cycles which may prevent the physical body from responding normally and well to the environment or the conditions where it is functioning at the present time.

Reprograming via spiritual laws, concepts, systems and needs is the only way to elevate this characteristic to the proper healthy, whole (holy) function. The subconscious functions, as expressed through astral-soul memories, serve all the other parts of the being, just as zeal serves all the other divine characteristics of the I Am expression.

Trance & Self-Hypnosis. Only through programing and mastering the automatic subconscious reflexes can some yogis and other spiritual adepts command their bodies to perform in seemingly unnatural ways. For example, it has been well documented that they can stop breathing, can live for a time without air, can lie on nails and other jagged sharp objects, can walk through fire unharmed, can impale their skin without bleeding.

157

Dreams, Hypnosis, Hallucinations. In these states most of us have had sensations that feel as real as physical ones. For example, if you have enjoyed swimming, with a variety of concomitant sensory pleasures, then in a dream or under hypnosis or through the hallucinatory effects of drugs you may be able to recall and to experience all the same sensations exactly as they occurred from those original memories. But this is not to approve of hypnosis or illicit drugs, for we do not approve.

These sensations are as real as the original ones because the memories are stored, sorted and organized in the subconscious. When some suggestion triggers this series it can cause a repeat performance which is difficult for some to delineate. Since the subconscious memory stores many soul experiences as well, sensations, memories, repetitions of this kind can be culled from episodes of past lifetimes, too.

This example was one of pleasure. But there are others we would need to reprogram and transmute through the zeal–enthusiasm center for the sake of bringing all conditions up to the standards our I Am Self requires. For only the good, productive, constructive and spiritual episodes are permitted to be stored permanently in this memory center, if it is to serve as an apostle/characteristic of the I Am Self; even if the reprograming procedure takes a thousand lifetimes or experiences.

Although the mind and the soul, like the body, may ingest ideas from varied sources, we must sort these out, digest them, assimilate them, and then eliminate them if necessary, allowing only the good substance to be stored in the memory-soul-astral body. Granted, all this may seem to be long and laborious and may take eons of time and tremendous patience. Nevertheless, if zeal is to serve all the other characteristics of the I Am Self, we must accept the function delegated to it and the design created for it.

As presented previously, there are two types of spiritual workers or two different types of responses to the implanting of the zeal aspect. Both need to reexamine all the previous nine consecutive steps or apostles to their Christ mission. They must accept the fact that by the very nature of either overzealousness or underzealousness they are expressing symptoms of not integrating the spiritual information of which they have partaken. Or they may be pushing too fast, too hard, too conscientiously into areas of expression for which they do not have yet all the proper tools and understanding.

At various stages of development, most of us react with: "I'm tired. The fire is gone. I can't absorb anything else. I can't concentrate on another new thing. I'm tired of opposing or struggling with those who reject this information." Personally and individually this is the time to stop. This is the period of reevaluation, when we must give time and due consideration to the digesting and the systematizing of all that has gone before. We do not partake of food or spiritual ideas twenty-four hours a day without resting, sleeping, absorbing, digesting, discarding, allowing the body to build and to restructure itself from the new substance we have eaten.

On the opposite side, however, there are those who think that spiritual students never should have such thoughts and feelings. They are apt to scold: "A spiritual person never should express such thoughts, whether they are true or false, because that is negative." This type constantly manufactures a false sense of enthusiasm for everything, no matter how minor or temporary. They are bombastic and overdramatic in their responses to the smallest, most insignificant details. When truly horrible events occur in the world—their own or the larger scene around them—they respond with a hearty laugh or a benign smile, saying: "That is good; for only good can occur in God's creations. It is a lesson, and good surely will come of it." The history of mankind and the Earth belies this attitude.

The overzealous represent those who have not taken time enough to digest and to discard the half-truths they have taken into their systems along with higher principles and cosmic laws. This point is extremely important and needs to be repeated frequently. Although well-intentioned, overzealous persons have a dangerous tendency to spread error conditions along with the newfound, to them, facts of spiritual life. Not only does this contribute to the downfall of the zealot but it can destroy the persons to whom the zealot transfers these half-truths with great passion.

If one speeds up the digestive phase, or neglects or ignores part of the elimination process, or does not allow sufficient time for assimilation, then one automatically transmits problems along with solutions which may turn out to be only partially workable and true.

The overzealous person usually considers every event, experience and thought to have some good merit. This type forgets the essential lesson nature examples, where it grows thorns, crusts, shells, indigestible skins and such alongside the delicate, nourishing parts of the fruits.

Developing our I Am expression is like growing a garden. We have to pluck from the memory storehouse certain situations (weeds) which

159

could be damaging and destructive. Willingly and totally we must consciously transmute them. We cannot allow these to exist and to be assimilated along with the growing shoots of truth and good. If we exercise such good common sense in the world of horticulture, how much more should we apply it to our worlds of mental, emotional, physical and soul expression?

Some who are overzealous, albeit ignorant of or lacking in spiritual experience, have been known to state bravely: "I can live with error; I just rise above it all. People with evil intentions don't faze me, because I am spiritual and feel only love for everyone. Nothing less than good can touch or affect me." Truly these people deceive themselves. If this were so, great masters, saints and millions of spiritually-minded, dedicated souls never would have been persecuted, threatened, crucified or burned at the stake.

The fact of the matter is that evil and error can overwhelm even the most staunch of spiritual workers. Those who deliberately and consciously allow themselves to remain in a situation or a relationship which is downgrading, false or error-ridden eventually are swept into the storms created by those conditions. As a result, often they lose temporarily the first stages of spiritual advancement.

Overzealousness is dangerous to both the person and the program or the particular cause being served. What follows usually is overconfidence. The zealot releases an uncontrollable and unrealistic passion for spreading incomplete knowledge and realization. All suffer for this, because his zeal contains distortion and lack of reality. In other words, the zealot often proposes certain ideas and plans which cannot be accomplished. Ridicule and eventually disillusionment naturally result.

Both of these types represent legitimate ways spiritual students approach the characteristic of zeal and enthusiasm. Those of the first group are honest enough, but lack full understanding and discernment of the many stages, levels and necessary repetitions which are the requirements of gradual evolvement of all twelve aspects of I Am Self functioning. Those of the second group unfortunately try to force themselves and others into this apostolic function prematurely or to overwork it out of proportion to the other eleven. To them this function is either the major supporting role to the I Am or equal and synonymous to its expression. Therefore, they push it to the front and center of the stage of action. Such overemphasis is not natural, nor is it proper order and peaceful harmony, in I Am development.

To birth the light body on Earth at this time in a normal, easy, pleasant and right manner requires divine procedures with order, harmony and compatible rhythm. Spirit forces nothing. Spirit constantly balances. Never is Spirit ashamed of opposites. Both ends of the spectrum eventually will serve the good that Spirit desires to have manifested. Cosmic activity provides for ups and downs, happy constructive periods and unpleasant destructive restructurings, positive and negative polarities, action and rest cycles, and so forth.

In working uncompromisingly for spiritual results, there is nothing of which we should be ashamed or afraid. It is not erroneous to require a down cycle or a rest period when we properly need it for further introspection, concentration, or to improve and to apply one of the other eleven functions of the I Am Self. For instance, we may have passed successfully through each of the twelve characteristics, only to find that a deeper level of understanding or some new nuance or facet requires additional time and development. It can enter the consciousness easily and logically; or it may come as a shock, that there is additional data or deeper application necessary. In either case we must stop to reevaluate. In that process there is a great deal of introspection and self-analysis. Thereby we lose temporarily a certain degree of enthusiasm.

But this response is perfectly natural. It is in proper order and it contains divine wisdom. It also allows for regrouping of all efforts, perhaps into a much higher and much more efficient manner than we have developed heretofore. If, by delving still deeper into greater spiritual understanding and better applications of all the divine assets at man's disposal, we can resolve many problems in a more satisfying manner, that in itself is worth the additional efforts and the essential cleansings. After these have set, enthusiasm and zeal return, because we have resolved the problems in a much higher level of consciousness and from a greater perspective, revealing more of the multifaceted interests of Spirit in all things.

To sum up, here are seven steps which are natural and normal to all of us in integrating the quality of zeal for I Am functioning: (1) loss of enthusiasm; (2) period of introspection; (3) realization of new facts; (4) deeper spiritual understanding; (5) still further cleansing of errors; (6) renewed dedication for the spiritual purpose and plan; (7) finally, an automatic return of true zeal. In the seventh step there are at least four degrees: (1) contentment; (2) happiness, then joy; (3) renewed enthusiasm for the original cause; (4) zeal.

How wonderful. How logical. How simple it all is on paper. Yet, how often each of us forgets and bemoans these necessary and spiritually correct steps of spiritual wisdom. Accept the fact that there is a swinging of moods, a rhythm in divine order and harmony. All things when spiritually motivated will occur at the right time and for the greatest good of all parts and persons involved. This is the very nature of Spirit Itself.

Go back to the first step, faith. If you have fear or worry that matters are not in divine order and harmony, and that only your personal intervention can alter those matters, then you have a lack of faith and wisdom. This then would require a period of retracing the spiritual growth patterns and going back to the first step of faith in God; and that, as a child of God, you eventually must expect only the best for your highest good and progress.

See now how this system works. When there is a block or a clog at any one step along the route, take the time—and don't begrudge it— to go back to the first building stone: faith. Travel through each step in sequential and proper order to get back to the original roadblock. Retracing the path in itself dissolves and eventually eliminates all blocks to spiritual evolvement.

Reviewing finally: during the birthing of the light body it is essential to know that enthusiasm and zeal occur when all other considerations are operating in the proper place and at the right time. To hold any feelings of guilt because of lack of enthusiasm is to deny this spiritual fact. Enthusiasm and zeal are natural by-products of right action, right programing at the right time and place in evolvement. As already described, zeal is automatic; just as its physical counterpart in the body, the functioning of the hypothalamus and the medulla oblongata for subconscious reflexes and astral-soul body reactions, is automatic. Enthusiasm and zeal occur automatically when everything in the life—all relationships, every attitude—is in divine order and harmony.

Lack of this spiritual function should be the signal that conditions are not what they seem; or what they will be or can be by greater efforts, more cleansings, further reevaluations, better balancings, and perhaps a needed rest cycle.

The manufacturing of zeal or forcing of enthusiasm when matters are not proper and correct in the life expression causes a burning-out, a false fire in the system. If the system—meaning all levels of expression: physical, mental, emotional and soul-astral—already is out of balance and is not functioning in an orderly way, applying greater pressure or energy in the already drained system will cause a blowout. Through the actual transaction of putting all conditions into order, zeal is the automatic consequence.

Most importantly, zeal and enthusiasm are the natural gauges for discerning how well all the other eleven characteristics of the I Am Self are positioned for proper functioning in the light body. The willing and wise spiritual student knows and accepts this as fact. Happily and gratefully those individuals work with Spirit's divinely ordered methods. They adjust what needs to be adjusted with quiet and determined thanks, expecting and eventually receiving the rewards of enthusiasm and zeal.

PHYSICAL DATA
Hypothalamus & Medulla Oblongata

The spiritual quality of zeal–enthusiasm externalizes via the third-eye chakra as the hypothalamus and the medulla oblongata, which are located at the base of the brain. (See Figures 10a and 10b.) *Hypo-* means *below*, so the hypothalamus lies below the thalamus and above the pituitary gland. Beneath the hypothalamus is the brain stem, which consists of the midbrain, the pons and the medulla oblongata. The hypothalamus and the medulla oblongata monitor and regulate the body's automatic functions and cyclic activities that are under subconscious control. These include heart rate, respiratory rate, temperature, water balance, appetite, and the sleep-wake cycle.

The hypothalamus carries out its functions by regulating the secretion of all pituitary hormones and by sending messages via the sympathetic and the parasympathetic nerves to all parts of the body. For example, when the hypothalamus senses that fluid levels are too high, it directs the pituitary gland to secrete less antidiuretic hormone, which causes the kidneys to eliminate more water via the urine. When blood passing through the hypothalamic temperature center is too warm, the hypothalamus sends out nerve signals to increase sweating and to dilate capillaries near the surface of the skin.

The hypothalamus regulates heart and respiratory rates by transmitting nerve impulses to cardiac and respiratory control centers in the medulla oblongata. From there, sympathetic or parasympathetic nerve messages travel to the heart and the lungs. Sympathetic nerve impulses increase heart and respiratory rates, whereas parasympathetic signals decrease them. The medulla oblongata also has centers which mediate

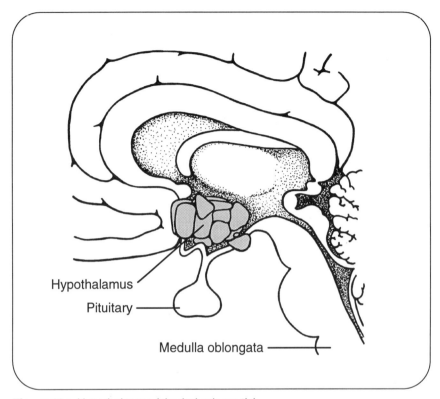

Figure 10a. Hypothalamus (shaded schematic).

the swallowing and the vomiting reflexes.

The reticular activating system is a loosely organized network of neurons located in the medulla oblongata, the pons, the midbrain and the hypothalamus. (See Figure 10b.) This system controls the sleep-wake cycle. It also controls the degree of mental alertness and clarity, as well as the overall energy level. Signals from the reticular activating system travel via the thalamus to the cerebrum, directing it and the mind to be awake, alert, drowsy, asleep, or to dream.

The hypothalamus regulates our mood by synthesizing and releasing beta-endorphin, which has morphinelike qualities. Beta-endorphin eliminates pain and produces feelings of well-being, peace and bliss. Physical exercise causes beta-endorphin release; hence the term "runner's high." However, the hypothalamus apparently also releases beta-endorphin when we laugh and when we feel love, joy and oneness with our I Am Self.

164

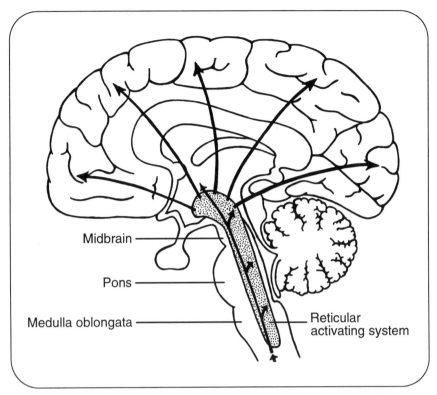

Figure 10b. Reticular activating system (arrows depict signal pathways).

Our mood also is regulated by centers in the brain stem which produce the neurotransmitters norepinephrine and serotonin. The rise and fall in the amount of these two transmitters modulates the changes of mood from elation to depression. Antidepressant medications work by increasing the concentration of norepinephrine and/or serotonin.

Imbalances in the zeal characteristic may cause lowered energy, from minor tiredness to chronic fatigue syndrome; insomnia (difficulty in initiating or maintaining sleep) or hypersomnia (excessive amounts of sleep and excessive daytime sleepiness); and mood disorders, the most serious of which are mania (undue elation and excitability) and depression.

Numerous physical factors also may be involved in the above conditions. Low energy may be caused by hypothyroidism, anemia, nutritional deficiencies or ingestion of toxic substances. There may be a genetic predisposition to mood disorders. Therefore, if problems persist or are severe, see your doctor, who will perform the necessary diagnostic tests and will prescribe appropriate treatment, including medication.

Whether there are physical causes or not, however, focus on the spiritual quality of zeal–enthusiasm. Analyze and reprogram any tendency you may have to be overzealous or underzealous. Visualize yourself as even-tempered, joyously taking things one step at a time. Give thanks unto Spirit for supplying you with just the right amount of energy in every situation.

COLOR VISUALIZATION
Rosy Pink

The color to which this divine characteristic of the I Am Self responds is rosy pink. Rosy, according to a dictionary, means *hopeful*. This condition is the natural response and the emotional reaction of the soul after it has reached the stage where everything is in divine order and harmony; and honest, balanced enthusiasm and zeal are expressed.

Rosy pink is warm, exciting, passionate with spiritual desires, filled to the brim with the supreme feeling of love for God. This love of the I Am Self is for divine laws, spiritual methods, the orderly course of the universe and of all in it.

It is a shade or two below the spectrum of blood red, which is the color of the next spiritual characteristic of regeneration and rebirth. Here again, by gradually working in shades and degrees, is the example of the orderly progression designed to birth the light body into the physical dimension.

Using the symbolism and the gentleness of pink roses you will stimulate the subconscious, such as in dreams and meditations; will reawaken soul memories tenderly, without shock, fear, retribution or vengeance. Think of your subconscious/soul record as a tiny, tight, pink bud. It contains the essence and the potential of all that has been grown and experienced before it developed on the stem of your Christ flowering. Gradually it gathers more and more energy, courage and strength. Slowly your soul records and memories open to your conscious mind petal by petal, event by event until the entire blossom of your past opens itself willingly and hopefully to the sun/Son light of your I Am Self.

SONG INSPIRATION
Zeal

Rushing through this life,
Always in a hurry,
Burning up with zeal,
I can't sleep, I only worry.

Too full or sometimes empty,
Too much or not enough,
Icy chills and burning fever;
Bouncing back and forth, back and forth, back and forth.

chorus
Zeal, zeal, the way I feel,
A source of joy that's always real.
Zeal, zeal, the way I feel,
Living with that inner thrill, that inner thrill, that inner thrill.

Gonna get my life in order,
Gonna feel a balanced zeal,
Gonna keep my energy flowing
And express the way I feel.

Taking time to smell the roses,
Taking time to sort things out;
Not intense but not deflated;
From within, not from without, not from without, not from
   without.

chorus
Zeal, zeal, the way I feel,
A source of joy that's always real.
Zeal, zeal, the way I feel,
Living with that inner thrill, that inner thrill, that inner thrill.

11. Regeneration

Metaphysical Interpretation: *Judas Iscariot*

Physical Data: *Reproductive System*

Color Visualization: *Ruby Red*

Song Inspiration: *Regeneration*

METAPHYSICAL INTERPRETATION
Judas Iscariot

After enthusiasm and zeal completely infuse our being, the next logical, sequential step is the inescapable desire to produce more of the same, to repeat the pattern, to share the good. We move from zeal into reproduction and creativity. Dictionary definitions for regeneration are: *spiritual renewal; to give, to gain, to grow new life.*

Misinterpretation of zeal, the immediately preceding step in the birth of the light body, presumes an active state. But, as it has been explained, zeal actually is a passive condition which cannot be forced. It cannot be consciously willed or manifested, because it is an automatic reflex when all other conditions are in the rightful place and order. Therefore, when this overwhelming sense of joy and spiritual passion infuses every thought, word and action it generates an active spiritual desire to reproduce more of the same, to bring forth or to create further spiritual ideas, compositions, new forms of life.

Spiritual seeds or ideas are always alive in the I Am individual; only they do not germinate into manifested actions each and every time there is a flow of inspiration. It takes a special combination of factors to germinate the new spiritual seed. So, the wise and patient I Am individual waits for the judicious moment, and does not expect a new child/manifestation to be born as a result of every feeling of divine love and action flowing through the consciousness and the life's services. There must be a trust in Spirit's overall plan to germinate the sperm/idea with the ovum/love flowing throughout mind, body and soul.

In the case of Mary, the mother of Jesus, she prepared herself as a virgin vessel by cleansing, understanding, accepting divine will; and expressing joy, thanks and zeal for her role as the womb/mother for Israel's Messiah. Until she had completed satisfactorily all the preliminary steps, she could not be given this commission.

Likewise, during Jesus' life many opportunities and needs presented themselves for him to manifest or to create the demonstrations of healing, supply, teachings, soul responsibilities and missions of others; and to fulfill long-awaited prophecies of the Hebrew people. But wisdom and patience prevented him from acting upon every single occasion. He responded discerningly, circumspectly, cautiously, prudently, lovingly, and with utmost deliberation.

Those in the Christ consciousness do not spill the seeds of their spiritual energies and ideas upon every occasion, or to prove the fertility of their minds and souls. Instead, they judge and weigh the merits of the time, the place, the worthiness and the receptivity of those involved. If they didn't they would empty the oil of their lamps, like the foolish virgins in Jesus' parable, and be spent and dried-up when the Christ within required them to give of their inner light and life force.

The temptations to spend spiritual life force are similar to and as great as those in the carnal or the physical sense. Usually they are for special and personal gratification, for pleasure and honor to the personality, for satisfaction of an immediate need, for the praise and the thanks involved. These temptations give no thought to the future consequences, to the karmic obligations of those involved, to the proper balance of all conditions in the total situation.

These same temptations relate to love and sex relationships, to political conditions and power plays, to spiritual leaders and those demonstrating psychic phenomena, to the creative arts and innovations, to those who produce and merchandise material goods and supplies. In each area there is the desire to reproduce after its own kind. If the service is according to divine principles and for the highest good of all involved, the regeneration is responsible and beneficial. Divine laws and spiritual activities flow through every aspect of life and have myriad levels of expression. Determining how to express the spiritual characteristic of regeneration is the responsibility of the I Am individual.

To repeat, Jesus as our way shower demonstrated this responsibility on many levels and in many different kinds of performances. Some of his acts were material and mundane if the occasion called for such. Not all of his demonstrations of regeneration were abstruse and of abstract teachings. Using the characteristic of creative life force by the I Am Self is a deliberate and conscious act, considering all consequences and karma of those who participate and eventually may be affected by it.

Since Judas Iscariot represents the faculties of this characteristic, we must examine deeply and from every complex angle what his particular role and function were in the Christ drama. Like each of the other apostles/functions, Judas/regeneration has its good potential and its dangerous error possibilities. The Christ/I Am Self alone must have total understanding of both sides of its inherent nature and total command of them.

The Judas aspect in us betrays (reveals) the real basic motivation, the rock-bottom level of self-control, from which each of us demonstrates. Jesus knew fully Judas' thoughts and motives, his weaknesses, and his desires for the Messiah to rule in Israel (the congregation of spiritual ideas and plans). In fact, Jesus allowed, even encouraged, Judas to perform the deed he contemplated. "Go, and go quickly, for what you have to do," he said resignedly at the Last Supper.

Without fulfilling the prophecies of thousands of years in Hebrew lore, the Messiah could not bring forth the renewed form, dedication, understanding and teaching. The crucifixion of the old was necessary to bring forth the resurrection of the light body. The mission of the Messiah was not to be king of a political state—which was what Judas and many others interpreted it to be—but to birth the light body for the race of man on Earth, to bring mankind back into fourth dimensional consciousness and vibrations.

Therefore, Jesus was in conscious control of this regeneration faculty, even though it involved the betrayal and the revelation of the error of Judas' (and those like him) interpretation of the Christ message and mission. If Jesus had not been in full control of all his apostles/characteristics, he could not have produced the resurrected, light-body form. Review each one of the apostolic steps:

(1) At the point where he permitted the betrayal and the crucifixion, Jesus had recruited and had gained *faith* (Peter) in who he was and why he had come into incarnation at that time and place in the history of man on Earth.

(2) He had tested himself on the *strength* and *steadfastness* (Andrew) to face dishonor, punishment, ridicule, disbelief, the sentences of heresy and death.

(3) His *love* (John) was firm and unimpeachable. "The Father and I are one. When you see the son, you see the Father [the I Am within]. When you see the Father, you actually are looking upon the son."

(4) In his own consciousness he experienced and prophesied openly the ordeal of the next few days of his life. With spiritual *wisdom*, he *judged* and *discerned* (James son of Zebedee) that there was no other way to prove man was capable at this level of his evolution of overcoming the last mortal enemy of death.

(5) Regardless of what he personally wanted, he submitted totally to the *will* (Matthew) of the I Am Self. "Not my will be done, but Thine."

(6) Nothing could stand in his way or stop the inevitable chain of events. Jesus demonstrated here *mastery* and *power* (Philip) over his

own fate. He would not be subject to the whims and the false commands and the ideas of any other being or element in his environment.

(7) With full confidence, he had the *image* (Nathanael) of the resurrected, light body. In his *imagination* he did not lose his personal identity, but continued to be an individualized child of God.

(8) Jesus *understood* (Thomas) consciously, without complicated rhetoric and theory, all the reasons history had unfolded as it had in the past; why people in the present were acting and reacting in the manners of that particular time and moment; and, above all, what was necessary for him to be and to do to bring forth the future pattern for mankind on Earth.

(9) He accepted the *system* and *orderliness* (James son of Alphaeus) of the events as they unfolded, and of the persons who wittingly and unwittingly played out the roles of their individual destinies. He permitted Judas to witness the consequences of his willful and stubborn deed. He warned his closest apostles that their spirits indeed were willing but their flesh was weak. He did not condemn those who condemned and persecuted him for what he must do. "Father, forgive them. They know not what they do." He was secure in his knowledge and in the orderliness of the divine manifestations. "Tear down this temple [body] and in three days I will build it anew."

(10) Having done all that he could or was permitted to do, and having taught all his apostles everything they could absorb for the time, he quietly and efficiently, with sufficient *zeal* and *enthusiasm* (Simon the Cananaean) if not mortal joy, set out to complete the mission which was then for him and is now for us.

(11) *Regeneration* and *re-creation of the life force within* (Judas Iscariot) of our spiritual, I Am beingness, the light body or fourth dimensional frequency form, is the mission of all of us.

(12) Yet to be achieved—and Jesus was well aware then that it might take another two thousand years for mankind to appreciate this—are the *elimination, denial, renunciation* (Jude Thaddaeus) of the race's error concept of death. After all, there is only one Life Force: God, everlasting Energy, eternal Creator. Nothing else must be permitted to have power over our minds, bodies and souls. "I am in the Father and the Father is in me. We are one."

Judas, Judah (one of the twelve tribes of Israel) and Jude (also called Thaddaeus, the twelfth apostle and Judas' counterpart/companion, the faculty of elimination, denial and renunciation) all mean the same thing:

confessor, revealer, betrayer. This characteristic reveals or betrays our true level of I Am manifestation. It confesses to the others how much progress we have made.

Iscariot means *man of the cities, man of hostile encounters, man of conveniences.* Cities represent collections of certain ideas and concepts in our consciousnesses. The hostile encounter is the final battle with ideas of death. Death is a convenient, albeit temporary, expedient. As modern slang goes, death is a cop-out. It is a temporary escape from our errors, aggravations, inability to solve our problems. In reality, death is only a transition to another set of circumstances where the problems, the errors and the aggravations manifest in another way.

The ability of man—made in the image and the likeness of our Parent Creator, God—to re-create, to renew, to regenerate is indeed a convenience, and serves us both on the mortal levels and through the immortal, I Am expressions. Reproduction on any level brings us honor and prestige. It satisfies our basic urges to repeat ourselves.

But we must be careful not to tempt this faculty into action before we are ready to see all the ramifications through to their final conclusions. The new children/images or works/products/services must be as rungs on a ladder for others to climb to the same place and honor we enjoy. Reproduction for self-satisfaction, self-glory, self-aggrandizement will destroy a creator. We cannot force God, Life Energy, to perform or to bring forth more of the same kind as ourselves just to please ourselves or to serve our personal needs and satisfactions.

Spirit acts upon us as we act upon It. This is the law; it does not change for individual or personal reasons or secret motives. Spirit, by Its very nature, serves all of Its creations equally. Therefore, in expressing Spirit by the I Am Self we must be careful in our thoughts and actions about demonstrating new talents, functions, roles or missions for this hierarchal program of evolution. Every one of the other eleven characteristics must be obedient to our divine commands and control before we put into motion this regenerating life force.

We must be ready to accept the fact that everything we think, say and do comes back to betray or to reveal exactly the state of our consciousness, the level of our accomplishments in achieving Christ status, the secret desires and talents we covet, and how far we really have climbed on the road to Christhood.

Our creative life force, the reproduction faculty in the spiritual as well as in the mortal man, is bound to re-create after its own kind. But mortal man has no control over the reproducing faculty for the light body. This function is a natural and automatic fusion after all the other faculties/characterizations are operative. Furthermore, there is a subtle but important parallel between the two apostolic characteristics of regeneration/Judas and divine will/Matthew.

The first six apostles/characteristics represent the involution of spiritual man into matter form. The second six are the evolutionary characteristics of earthbound personality form returning to I Am expression. The fifth step in involution is divine will, represented by Matthew. The fifth step in evolution is regeneration, represented by Judas. As explained, divine will correlates in the physical mechanism and body systems through respiration, the breath of life, the will to live; regeneration correlates in the physical body with the reproductive system.

Without the will to live and the ability to breathe, the form reproduced cannot exist in the environment where it has been created. To the uninitiated in spiritual laws, this free will appears to be according to the whim and the desire of the individual personality. But to those familiar with the cosmic principles involved, free will equates to the willingness to breathe life, if it is in accordance to the divine will of the control factor for that individualization of God, the I Am Self.

In fact, one of Judas' major complaints about the behavior of the Christ man Jesus concerned the disbursement of the common purse. Judas kept the purse, yet would pilfer money from it. He also objected to Mary of Bethany using costly perfume to anoint the Master. He argued that it should have been sold and the money given to the poor. Matthew the tax collector, both literally in the apostolic sense and figuratively in the characteristic sense, represented to Judas/regeneration an anomaly.

Putting it into generalized mortal philosophies today, the average male and female in copulating believe they choose life force to be created. It is beyond their comprehension or acceptance that it is the I Am Self of the form they are helping to create who, using its divine and free will, makes the decision to be born, to breathe, to live. Until reaching a spiritual understanding of the trinity principles of Life Force operating on the mortal as well as the cosmic planes, man erroneously credits his own limited powers and will as the decisive factors in life or death.

So it was wrongly conceived by the apostle Judas. He adulterated spiritual principles and usurped responsibilities beyond those the Christ man had given him. Instead of submitting to and respecting the divine will in his function to help regenerate and bring forth the new Christed man through Jesus, the mortal man, he forced his mortal will and interpretations upon the Christ mission of Jesus. His actions did not abort the mission, for mortal will cannot abort spiritual will. It can only succeed in rechanneling it through another area or byroad.

Judas' acceptance of thirty pieces of silver (a man-made exchange for energy and valuables) to reveal the whereabouts of Jesus (representing spiritual causes and concepts) further substantiates this point. Thirty is a symbol for the Trinity, Father-Mother-Child. This is the regenerative activity of Life Force, God. According to divine principles, Idea (Father) coupled with Energy (Mother) produce Man-ifestation. However, mortal man believes male and female create life; and that the spirit of the child, only whose form they help to conceive, is not to be considered.

Eventually Judas recognized his error and denounced his deed. He threw the thirty pieces of silver back to the priests—who are supposed to represent and to support spiritual laws and principles—and attempted to transmute his act by choosing death.

In fact, as an added emphasis to this spiritual system of birthing the light body on Earth, Judas, who objected to the rightful function of Matthew, was replaced by one called Matthias, a name derived from Matthew and which also represents *divine will*. After Jesus' ascension the community of Christ disciples cast lots to select Matthias, who was an incarnation of the spiritual master St. Germain, Chohan or Director of the Sixth Ray of Transmutation in our solar system government.

Transmutation (elimination of the old and transformation into the new) is the passive polarity to the active polarity/companion of regeneration. These dual steps are the final characteristics and functions to be incorporated into man's evolutionary pattern to return to the Christ state of consciousness and the I Am, light body. They interact, and are as inseparable as any other of the six pairs or twelve divine characteristics of the I Am Self.

Twist and turn as he might, there is no way man can force Spirit and cosmic laws and functions to obey his ideas, interpretations and mortal will. His own lack of understanding and ability to imagine the Christed way is what betrayed Judas for himself and those thought patterns or individuals like him. It is hard to believe that Judas' intention was to destroy the mission and the purpose of the Messiah, as interpreted and exampled by Jesus. The devilish ideas that entered into Judas were those thoughts and concepts which convinced him, and undoubtedly thousands like him in those days, that physical force and reformation were better solutions than the spiritual ones being offered by Jesus.

Few of the disciples, not Judas alone, actually comprehended the ramifications of Jesus' teachings. None of them had reached a high enough spiritual level in externalizing their I Am Selves to comprehend his lessons and demonstrations. None of them were able to reproduce according to the divine pattern he was setting before them. Thus, Judas betrayed their limitations as well as his own. The creative life force surging through him without restraint and patience allowed him to take matters into his own hands and to force the Christ Self to take the form he willed it to take.

Mortal man, as Judas in the drama of Jesus' life, betrays man's limited and physical solutions to spiritual conditions. In spite of Judas having forced the issue at that time, the spiritual solutions still have not regenerated or re-formed man's life on this planet. Not until there is a spiritual regeneration of the total man can the problems, the pain, the disharmonies be fully dissolved. Mortal will and strictly man-made regenerative solutions merely reassemble the form the problems take. Only spiritual regeneration and the etheric form of man, the light body, can replace what is undesirable and unworkable.

Judas betrayed his limited knowledge and acceptance of the powers and the potentialities of the Christed man. He succeeded only in reproducing a temporary solution to a problem that is twenty-six million years old, dating from the final fall of man into the third dimension. It remains for the followers of the Christ pattern, through Jesus, to remedy those mistaken ideas. The cosmic laws and systems cannot be bent or changed to satisfy any immediate need or whim.

Jesus, representing our Christ Selves, remained steadfast to his mission, unafraid of temporary diversions, undaunted by the betrayal of any one of the twelve apostles/characteristics. "Not my will but Thine be done." In the tomb it was up to him to manifest the light body for the resurrection demonstration. The subconscious memories, the soul records, the astral body during those three days of darkness re-formed and regenerated the physical molecular structure and birthed the light body. This form did not change totally. For the new must be formed out of the old, the parent form.

Neither was the light-body form an exact duplicate of the parent-mortal form or frame recognizable as Jesus of Nazareth. For even his most beloved female disciple was unable to recognize him on Easter morning. Mary of Magdala confronted him with, "Gardener, do you know what they have done with the body of my Master?" Two disciples traveling with him for miles on the road to Emmaus recounted to him the events of the crucifixion in Jerusalem, not recognizing him by voice or manner until supper that evening; whereupon he dematerialized.

When the eleven apostles were praying in a locked room, Jesus appeared in his light body in their midst. In other words, three-dimensional structural forms no longer were obstacles to him in his fourth dimensional, light body. But they thought it was his "ghost," his astral shadow, and still did not understand the resurrection of the Christ body of the spiritual, I Am Self.

Nothing of our personal and mortal will can create the light body. The crossing-out of the mortal ways and concepts is the only true road open to man of Earth. Each has his own mission, purpose, function and individuality. No two children of our Father-Mother God are alike or can duplicate one another. Since we must reproduce after our own kind and nature, some of this individuality of the I Am Self is now, at this moment, broadcasting out from the consciousness of the mortal expression evolving back into immortal, I Am beingness.

The scars and the wounds of our mortal records will be borne on the light-body form, just as Jesus' wounds of crucifixion were visible to his disciples upon his resurrection. Our light bodies and the spiritual functions of the fourth dimensional existence are not totally alien to our experiences and levels of manifestation throughout Earth history of the last two hundred and six million years. Man will not reproduce as angels or as animals. We will reproduce the light bodies of the race of man.

The Judas characteristic—the creative life force and reproduction faculty of our I Am Selves—will reveal, cannot do otherwise, that which we are, that which we have attained, that which we must work to improve and to transmute before the final fusion of all twelve characteristics, functioning in balance and harmony for the I Am Self.

This final fusion and the full demonstration of the light-body expression are not a one-lifetime effort for man of Earth. It has taken hundreds of lifetimes throughout the solar system to regain the reproductive stage. Many Earth experiences, many astral plane lessons, many other planetary explorations have been involved in the learning and the relearning processes. But at each turning point of our return to I Am Self beingness, this inexorable function of Judas—the creative life force–regeneration–reproduction—has revealed how much we have learned, how willing we are to be in that I Am, light body.

179

Those who are of the one hundred and forty-four thousand light workers expecting to demonstrate this fourth dimensional body for the hierarchal plan during this Mark Age must accept that there will be thousands of experiences, trials and errors, betrayals and false pregnancies before they can birth the light body into this Earth plane frequency via the personality structures they are expressing here and now.

In the wheel of repetition—trial and error, cause and effect—it is always the Judas characteristic and purpose to create after its own kind and level of development. Creative life force can reproduce only after its own kind: the seed/idea and the egg/soul. Only what has been fused in each one's mind and soul can be reproduced in the life's experiences and services.

If the seeds (ideas) are good and the soil (soul) is properly furrowed, fusion will occur. Spirit will breathe life into each seed and the fruit will form on the vine. The fruit of all these labors and preliminary steps is the light body. Should the seeds and the soil be lacking in the proper ingredients, the fruit may not form; if it does, it will not ripen. Through trial and error, cause and effect, we gain comprehension of the system. We begin again, the better for the experiences. But it is impossible to bring forth fruits better than the conditions of the seeds (ideas) planted into the soil (soul) of our individual consciousness and actions.

In the reprograming of creative life force–regeneration, we must pay some attention to the Earth plane ideas of man's sexual nature. Presently the race ideas and patterns are so overwhelmingly powerful and predominant that spiritual conceptions of reproduction and regeneration are extremely difficult to anchor into the conscious mind.

The sex organs in the human form have been developed in order to reproduce the species after its own kind. The sex act never was intended to be strictly for pleasure, power or self-appreciation. True, the pleasure sensations are part of the normal process, because all things in the natural kingdoms of this environment should be pleasurable and performed with willingness and desire when enacted in harmony with the original purpose. But pleasure for pleasure's sake never was the basic intent and purpose, neither on the mortal nor on the spiritual level.

One may deduce quickly that the misdirections of this God-given creative life force have delayed extensively—for hundreds, possibly thousands, of incarnations—the evolution of mankind out of the third dimensional experience back into his rightful, fourth dimensional frequency expression, the light-body form. We need only reexamine customs, laws, religious doctrines, national mores, even war cries, which have been formulated and based on misinterpretation and misdirection of the purposes of reproduction after its own kind. Whole structures in society have been built and perpetuated, have become the conditions for lifestyles, have been the cause of wars by the heirs of certain groups. There have been tribal wars, family feuds, national differences instilled in man to perpetuate his own kind. Certain souls have been bound, even on the astral planes, to bands of race or color or sociological patterns.

The limited knowledge that there is some special ingredient inherited from parent to child—the Earth concept of the divine right of kings, of the direct heir to fortunes, of family honor and tradition—has instigated horrendous battles and agonizing acts of less-than-human, let alone spiritual, qualities. Racial patterns and ideologies have condoned such behavior for eons. Human values and conditions are perpetuated. Spiritual laws and interpretations of cosmic patterns are ignored, and even ridiculed. The spiritual person birthing the light body fights upstream against this strong current of human thought patterns.

All that such mortal analyzing and thinking really accomplish is to deny that each individual equally is a child of God, the supreme Creator and eternal Life Force. There is a refusal to acknowledge that the human parents, the family group, the tribes, the nations and the religious sects only are vehicles through which all of God's creations of individual expressions may experience and express for only one life episode. One lifetime in no way may reflect all facets of the divine heritage and status or conditions of that child.

When this spiritual attitude predominates on Earth and when sex is used for proper reproductive purposes, most of the miseries in human, mortal, Earth-type living will be alleviated. But these concepts are revealed only through the regeneration of the mind and the revitalization of the race's purpose for existing or having explorations here on this planet and in this third dimension. Since this is rather a harsh and advanced teaching, those of lower levels of development, intentions or repatternings do not understand it easily. However, through repetition of these truths on higher levels in order to birth the light body, eventually the message and the lessons are realized; even if it has taken, and still may take, thousands of experiences and thousands of incarnations.

Each one must assume individual responsibility for this reprograming into I Am consciousness. Even though the whole race consciousness creates a thought atmosphere that is like an overpowering current in a stream, each individual must swim through it on his own. The group as a whole does not carry the individual. But each individual contributes to the overall group pattern and inherent traits.

Once spiritual truths are revealed to our conscious minds—Jesus teaching Judas and the other apostles—we each are responsible for our own actions. The longer we misuse or ignore spiritual facts, the more we develop and manifest negative karma. We reproduce according to those patterns and levels of understanding and experience. The more times we insist on returning to the error concepts, the harder it is to throw off, to eliminate, to renounce those acts and thoughts, because we keep reinforcing them on the lower, sensual, mortal levels. Sooner or later, we are obliged to accept the spiritual laws and standards for expressing mind, body and soul. When we do accept them, we shall re-create according to those higher standards and thought forms.

PHYSICAL DATA
Reproductive System

The spiritual quality of regeneration–creative life force manifests via the regenerative chakra as the male or the female reproductive organs, which are needed for the procreation of the race of man as long as he functions in a third dimensional or physical body on Earth. Male reproductive organs include penis, scrotum, testes, a duct system, prostate gland, seminal vesicles, and bulbourethral glands. (See Figure 11a.) Female reproductive organs include vagina, uterus, fallopian tubes, ovaries and breasts. (See Figure 11b.)

In the male, sperm or reproductive cells are produced in the testes, which are two small ovoid structures that are suspended from the body wall and enclosed in a sac, the scrotum. Each sperm carries twenty-three chromosomes containing genes or hereditary factors that are transmitted from one generation to the next. With ejaculation during sexual intercourse, a duct system carries sperm from the testes through the erect penis into the woman's vagina. This duct system consists of the epididymis, the seminal duct, the ejaculatory duct and the urethra. Accessory glands form seminal fluid that is added to the sperm coming from the testes. These glands include the seminal vesicles, the prostate gland and the bulbourethral glands. Together, sperm and seminal fluid are called semen, from the Latin word for *seed*.

In the female, each of two almond-shaped ovaries contains approxi-

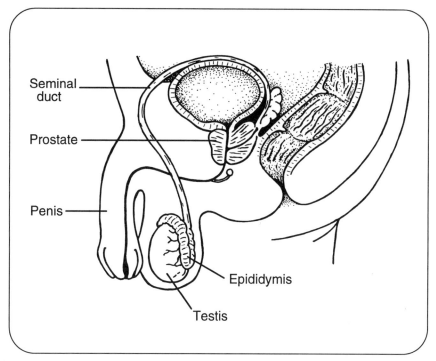

Figure 11a. Male reproductive system.

mately two hundred and fifty thousand ova or eggs, each of which has twenty-three chromosomes. During every menstrual cycle of about twenty-eight to thirty-two days, one ovum is released at about mid-cycle and is swept into one of the two fallopian tubes that are attached to the pear-shaped uterus or womb. If no sperm have been introduced into the vagina during sexual intercourse, and therefore no sperm have traveled up into the uterus and the fallopian tubes, fertilization or fusion of one sperm with the ovum does not occur. After about fourteen days, the lining of the uterus, which has grown in preparation for pregnancy, is shed, causing menstrual bleeding for about three to five days.

If fertilization does take place, however, the combined forty-six chromosomes begin directing the growth of an embryo. After about nine days, the developing embryo becomes embedded completely in the lining of the uterus. By eight to nine weeks, all twelve physical systems have begun to develop. The embryo, now called a fetus, typically grows within the uterus for another seven months. At birth, contractions of the muscular walls of the uterus propel the baby out of the womb, through

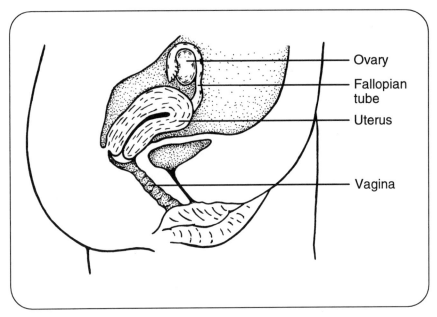

Figure 11b. Female reproductive system.

the vagina that now functions as a birth canal, and out of the mother's body. Milk produced by the mother's breasts or mammary glands provides nourishment for the newborn infant.

Errors and misapplications of the spiritual quality of regeneration may lead to diseases of the reproductive organs. In males, these include inflammation of the urethra, epididymis and testes; inflammation, enlargement and cancer of the prostate; impotence; and lowered sperm count. Female reproductive disorders include vaginal infections; pelvic inflammatory disease; uterine fibroids; ovarian cysts; irregular, painful or heavy menstrual periods; infertility; cysts, infections and benign growths of the breasts; and cancer of the uterus, ovaries or breasts. Both men and women may contract sexually transmitted diseases such as gonorrhea, syphilis, chlamydial infections, genital herpes and AIDS.

With disorders like cancer and AIDS, even though one applies holistic treatment, full healing of the physical body may not manifest in the current lifetime. Instead, final healing may come with death or transition to the higher astral planes, where any remaining soul errors may be reviewed, reprogramed and regenerated, and where the light form is birthed. Then, in a future life, one may birth the light body on Earth.

COLOR VISUALIZATION
Ruby Red

Ruby red is vivid, sharp, natural, bold; is often called true red or blood red. Blood is associated with the reproductive system, with the process of birth, and with spiritual regeneration.

In the lesser stages of man's evolution, priests spilled the blood of the sacrificial lamb to symbolize that pain and death of one form of living make way for rededication and rebirth into a new and higher form. Jesus at the Last Supper gave his disciples wine, saying: "This is my blood of the covenant, which is poured out for many. . . . I will not drink again of the fruit of the vine [blood or life force of the physical form] until that day when I drink it anew in the kingdom of God [I Am Self dominion]." Clearly, Jesus was indicating he would not manifest or reappear at the Second Coming in physical, mortal form, but through creative life force (spiritual blood), in the light body, the fourth dimensional frequency form.

The female sheds blood each month at the end of her menstrual cycle. She sheds the old lining of the uterus (the old form) before forming a new one. Then, if the sperm (idea) fertilizes the ovum (soul), blood will carry nourishment to regenerate the new creation (manifestation of mind and soul).

When I was in Switzerland at the Matterhorn on June 9, 1975, Sananda used the red ruby stone symbolically to project new images for the re-formation of Europe. The red ruby stone, he said, symbolizes his blood, which he as Jesus gave to purify the physical form of man, the third dimensional body. By his crucifixion and the giving of blood, the physical form of man on Earth became purified.

Now this form is to be decrystallized, regenerated, absorbed by the pure form of the I Am, light body. Sananda/Jesus channeled these words: "I ask that you see all in symbology in this instance, as explained through my channel Nada-Yolanda, and not take the literal explanation that so long has kept man bound in the physical and mortal concepts. For now the fourth dimensional consciousness and the I Am Self must dissolve all that you have held and have worked with and evolved out of. It has served its good purpose until now. Now release it and become new, renewed." Be reborn.

SONG INSPIRATION
Regeneration

Moving, moving the spiritual life force
Each beat of our heart, each breath that we take.
Growing, growing the spiritual life force,
We are made new, we regenerate.
Generating new life in me,
All that I am intended to be;
Creating a new possibility,
Born again, I'm born again.

Loving, loving each one the other
As each has its moment, each has its birth.
Being, being the spiritual life force,
Working together for a spiritual Earth.
Generating new life for mankind,
As our good fruits ripen we bear in mind
We're creating what we in the future shall find.
Born again, we're born again.

Spinning, spinning the spiritual life force
In all forms of life that dwell in this place.
Weaving, weaving the patterns of new life,
Creating a new world for a spiritual race.
Generating new life for us all,
The strong and the weak, the great and the small.
To all of creation we send out this call:
Be born again, be born again.
Born again, I'm born again.
Born again, we're born again.
Born again, be born again.

12. Elimination

Metaphysical Interpretation: *Jude Thaddaeus*

Physical Data: *Urinary System & Colon*

Color Visualization: *Violet*

Song Inspiration: *Elimination*

METAPHYSICAL INTERPRETATION
Jude Thaddaeus

The final step in the birth of the light body is to renounce and to eliminate the old form. This is a denial, without any regrets or retention of subconscious conditions, of the mortal coil around which third dimensional thinking and actions are woven.

The last act any newborn performs is to shuck off the shell or the birth sac upon which it has been totally dependent until regeneration was completed. Take a lesson from the animal kingdom. If the fully formed chick in its shell, because of any weakness in its development, cannot discard the shell by its own power and will, it is imprisoned in it and destroyed by it. In this way nature provides the newborn with its first challenge of survival in the new environment. Without gaining confidence and mastery it really cannot perform its other functions.

This provision is just as necessary for the race of man in the development and the birth of the light-body form in its earthbound sac or shell. This is the final step or decision of mortal man: to shuck off Earth-type thinking, habits, customs, race patterns, limited and expedient philosophies in favor of unknown, new and higher spiritual activities, responsibilities and codes.

More than ever it is evident during the last stage of evolvement that we are concerned with six pairs of functions: three pairs or six separate involuting characteristics plus three pairs or six separate evoluting characteristics (see chart on page 78). As with the other five pairs, the last dual set in our process of birth—Judas Iscariot (regeneration–creative life force–reproduction) and Jude Thaddaeus (elimination–renunciation–denial)—is as inseparable as the two sides of one coin.

Both Jude and Judas, in the literal translations, mean: *confessor or revelator of the I Am consciousness; praise of God and the I Am Self (Yahweh).* Jude, the apostle/characteristic of elimination, is surnamed Thaddaeus, meaning: *warmhearted, loving, tender, courageous, fearless.* In addition, he has been called the brother or the son of James; thus closely related, and with the strongest possible ties, to: *he who supplants, brings to an end, recompenses and rewards.*

Through this combination of names (the inherent nature), we know we have come to the end of our preparations and must fearlessly, tenderly, lovingly praise the I Am within and reveal fully its nature and purpose through our consciousness and acts.

But in order to allow this form of the I Am Self—Yahweh, as the Christ Self is called in the Old Testament—to have independent life and to express with free will, it is unconditionally necessary to cut the umbilical cord which bound it to the womb where it was protected and nourished. This womb, our physical body and mortal acceptance, served during gestation and regeneration. But now the characteristics and the functions of the I Am state of consciousness are fully ready to be tested. They are to be free from the body of Earth plane conditions.

For too long has mortal man considered elimination/renunciation/denial of the old conditions as a symptom of negativity, as an unkindness, as lacking in positive and loving thoughts. It has nothing to do with these things. Neither is it to be feared, shunned or shamed, any more than the mother and the newborn child would think and feel such at the cutting of the umbilical cord.

Elimination is the natural, logical process and the final necessary step of the I Am Self in calling together all its twelve divine functions. If courage is lacking, if love for freedom and independence is withheld, then the old relationships, thought forms, conditions of existence remain. In effect, they will strangle the newborn and thus destroy any chance of its survival in the new life form.

There is a time for living and a time for dying. In a very real sense we are reborn each day as that day provides us with new opportunities and circumstances. In the same way, each night we die or remove ourselves from present conditions in order that we may be born anew the next day and face that new day refreshed and rested.

There is a time for learning and a time for practicing what we have learned. The infant grows to be a child, the child to be an adult. The interests and the activities at each level of our growth have to change. We leave, discard, break away from, eliminate one level of our activities in order to enter into new and higher ones, to experience other challenges and opportunities. These observations of the natural laws on Earth are meant to give us food for thinking in spiritual ways and for understanding what seems to be unknown to our conscious, mortal systems.

If we have the inability or the lack of desire to discard, to destroy, to denounce or to eliminate unwanted, unproductive, unnourishing aspects and situations with which we have been associated and which we have ingested into our minds, souls and bodies, the results are disease of the body, disharmony in the mind, imbalance in the soul development. Inertia and apathy—no matter on which level they express: mind, body or soul—stem from fear of death. Death, as the apostle Paul already has told us, is the last enemy. Fear of death—with its misinterpretation as oblivion and total obliteration—keeps mankind shackled to the old ways and the familiar codes.

The very purpose of the Christ demonstration by Jesus for the race of man was to prove the resurrection of the light body; to eliminate the concept of death, as erroneously defined; to replace or to supplant the misguidance of the old teachings with the new testament of life eternal. For two thousand years priests of the Christ teachings and demonstrations have skirted, if not outright ignored, the core of the crucifixion–resurrection drama. The essence of Jesus' initiation was to remove fear of death and to replace it with love of life.

Until each child of God at this twelfth step eliminates the old concepts and supplants them with the new, he or she will not be able to birth the light body of the I Am Self. Recognize unconditionally, however, that the death of the physical body *is not necessary* to birth the light body. Unfortunately, this does not mean that the pain of transmuting mind, body and soul is not as great as what Jesus personally experienced on the cross. The way is not easy or simple. Man of Earth in his perversity took care of that.

Take comfort in the last words Jesus spoke in his mortal shell or sac: "Father, into Thy hands I commend my spirit." The *Father* of which Jesus the man spoke is the I Am Self (Sonship aspect of the Trinity). *Thy hands* refers to the manipulative and the management powers and characteristics of this divine Self. The word *commend* is defined in the dictionary as: *to commit to one's care, to praise, to recommend. My spirit* is the creative life force which is unique, individual, personal and eternal. It cannot die; it only can be re-formed, born anew.

Examine how on every level man learns to transmute and to work with this elimination faculty:

PHYSICAL. The food we eat and the water we drink go through a process of assimilation and then elimination. Some of the elements in these essential ingredients are unusable or unfit for total assimilation into our systems, so nature provides for their elimination. For example, the colon (large intestine) and the urinary system (kidneys, ureters, bladder and urethra) remove waste matter or pollutants. Some things we deliberately take into our systems. But in many instances the environment forces us to absorb unwanted matter, so our natural body functions are developed to eliminate such automatically. By this wondrous function it is obvious that we are not required to hold on to everything to which we are exposed or which we inadvertently ingest.

MENTAL. We learn facts and information in school. Our parents and society teach us many things according to their ideas and customs. We observe and experience infinite lessons through friends, business associates, training sessions, the creative efforts of others, and in our social exchanges. These by no means indicate we are to accept and to be guided in our thoughts, actions and comments by every single one of them.

In the first place, many of them contradict others. Common sense tells us to weigh their value, to judge their merits and to discern their demerits. Man-made proclamations of truth usually are the result of one particular, usually limited, point of view and are not based necessarily on cosmic laws and principles. Spiritual teachers invariably suggest that when in doubt you do nothing, form no firm opinion, seek more evidence; but until all the facts are in, keep your final opinion on the shelf.

EMOTIONAL. In early childhood we formed many attachments which no longer suit our development and progression into adulthood. A crush on a school friend, for example, is hardly the only criterion on which to base future love relationships, marriage vows or the role of parenthood. Certain relationships are well and good for the time and in the place where we are temporarily involved. But they do not serve us well always when we need to move ahead, or outside of that group of circumstances. There is no reason to feel ashamed when we outgrow a relationship or replace it with something more lasting, satisfying and productive.

It is not wrong to admit that a relationship has worn out. It is much more responsible to be able to renounce such when the interchanges no longer work for the mutual good and growth of all parties involved. There should be no guilt in a dead relationship and in relinquishing old ties. Naturally, we should fully recognize and accept the lessons we learned; and, with thanksgiving offered, we should distill all the good the relationship had to offer in every situation and emotion. But when the form it requires has become outmoded it is time to let go and to replace it with something better. Sometimes, and this is painful and difficult, it is necessary to let go before the replacement appears.

SOUL. There are some individuals who keep repeating the same patterns over and over; they carry them from relationship to relationship, situation to situation, lifetime to lifetime. Generally this type is incapable of discerning the patterns. Through overcare, possessive love and selfishness, fear, hatred, jealousy, competitiveness (which means a lack of self-worth and individuality), these persons are blind to the cause of their problem patterns. Their thoughts and emotions about those patterns create a force field which causes the same situations to be repeated again and again.

Truly they suffer. They seemingly cannot escape the very circumstances and conditions which hurt them. They hold on to them. For in them is the familiarity which spells, to their ways of thinking, life. They fear that if they let go of the individuals who hurt them, the conditions which spoil them, life will end. The enemy is not the individuals or the conditions which plague them, but death; at least the interpretation of death which has been allowed to persist on this planet: oblivion and obliteration of life.

But there is no such thing as death. There only is transformation or transmutation or translation into another series of experiences. Elimination, renunciation, denial are functions of living, not preludes to dying. They are as necessary to the spiritual child of God as they are to the child of man in matter form.

The Christ within, the I Am Self, is living. It is now and it always shall be. Eliminating and renouncing anything less than the right to express as the child of the living God, the I Am individuality, finally delivers us to the light of that expression. It allows the light body to flow through, to dominate totally and to control everything that comes into mind, body and soul. With the spiritual faculty of elimination we must renounce and deny every thought, desire, relationship and condition contrary to the eternal laws of our Parent God.

We must eliminate from the soul all past associations and memories which do not serve a properly balanced continuity of evolutionary services and functionings with the Christ body of mankind, the etheric or spiritual activities of the race. Here are just a few examples of how soul patterns may express from lifetime to lifetime on the Earth plane:

Male-Female Polarities. Some are conditioned to enjoy the functions of one gender or another; or, by certain sociological circumstances, are taught to accept one or the other more favorably. The person in I Am consciousness recognizes the equal opportunities, necessities, functions of each; and prefers neither one nor the other. In fact, the spiritual or cosmic person is simultaneously idea (male) and manifesting agent (female); and, fusing them together, demonstrates (procreates) the I Am Self in thought, word and action.

Sex. Some try to use the sex act mainly to please others or themselves, or to express power of self or over others. In any case, this ploy is an attempt to enslave others in one way or another. Invariably, however, it boomerangs. Those who attempt to use sex for anything but procreation of the race are to one degree or another enslaved by sex.

Superiority. This pattern is very subtle, because it manifests in many ways. Some are conditioned to believe there are superior races, religions, nations, genders, professions, creative talents or age groups. If all things are created of Spirit, and Spirit resides in all things, how can there be any one form or manifestation superior to another? Each has a place and a purpose, a special function, and a need to perform or to perfect that.

Mortal man, by these erroneous concepts and codes, has imprisoned himself in this dimension and has repeated endlessly these patterns. He not only has imprisoned or has suppressed others of the race because of their religion, creeds, color, national background and customs but has locked himself onto the wheel of repetition. In fact, via the law of cause and effect he may be forced to re-create or to reexperience the same conditions he imposes on others. For instance, if as a white person he has enslaved and has despised those in black bodies, he may return in another incarnation in a black skin so as to experience that which he allowed to fester in his thoughts and actions.

Only by eliminating, renouncing and denying such negative, unworthy, destructive patterns can man re-form and rebuild new and desirable ones. When lessons are thoroughly learned, when karmic conditions are totally balanced, Spirit eliminates the circumstances and the blueprints by which they exist. The manifestations or the forms Spirit creates are not eternal. Spirit is eternal. The spiritual consciousness of the I Am Self provides whatever vehicles are required for teaching the soul its proper lessons.

Therefore, we should not fear or shun elimination and renunciation of certain body forms and personalities. They are temporary measures through which spiritual purposes are effected. The I Am Self does not destroy the individuality of itself; it merely re-forms the vessel for a particular dimension or environment where it wishes to have experiences.

As a group, the race of man has participated in living experiences on this Earth and in this solar system for two hundred and six million years. During that time there has occurred the involution of the light-body forms into matter. For the last twenty-six million years the race on Earth has been evolving back to the light body from the material, human form. This reawakening or rebirth is the present hierarchal plan of the spiritual government of our solar system, culminating now in these Latter Days or the Mark Age period.

It is urgent that in these forty years (from 1960 to approximately 2000) of the Mark Age program, man of Earth accept the true meaning of death: denial and renunciation of one form or vessel in order that the Spirit within re-creates and re-forms a new and higher one.

Jesus, as Earthman's way shower, has demonstrated the pattern. That was his final act as the Prince of this planet for the solar system government. Dramatically, through twelve hand-picked apostles, he diagramed the acts we must perform individually and collectively. He spoke these words as guidelines for all who will follow him: "These things I do, you shall do; yes, even greater things." This statement is both literal and figurative. There is no death. There is only life, through transmutation and rebirth.

Putting on purple robes of rulership has been a signal that a person is favored by his peers or by God to rule over others. In the metaphysical sense, a king refers to rulership of the conscious mind over one's thoughts and activities, while a queen rules the subconscious. Before the I Am Self can rule all thoughts and affairs (birth the light body fully), the majesty and the dominion of our conscious-subconscious being must be unthreatened and unimpeachable. Man of Earth has been struggling toward this goal for twenty-six million years on this planet, on other planets in our solar system and on many dimensions, including the astral planes. So, these are not the efforts of one or several lifetimes, civilizations, eras or hierarchal plans.

Jesus alone on this planet, since Atlantis, has demonstrated the full union of mind, body and soul with the Christ Self. As that pattern maker he has established the overall drama of this struggle. His life in that incarnation gives the guidelines for every question and crisis in our own return to Christhood.

For instance, at this twelfth and final step in evolving back into I Am status we are liable to become overconfident and consider that only an intellectual understanding of this treatise is sufficient to complete the birth of our light body and to express totally the I Am consciousness. Yet there are several scenes in Jesus' passion play which exhort us to work and to rework, to pray without ceasing, for the birthing to be completed. Birth is not only fertilization, gestation, release from the womb and cutting of the umbilical cord, but it is consciously, independently breathing, feeding and acting as a separate individual.

Even before the crucifixion Jesus demonstrated that there were occasions when the Christ or I Am Self superseded the mortal, third dimensional body. He walked on water. He dematerialized in the midst of a threatening crowd. He healed the sick. He multiplied the loaves and fishes to feed the five thousand. He was transfigured on the mount, displaying to three of his apostles two of his past incarnations, Elijah and Moses.

In spite of these magnificent demonstrations of the light body before his trial and crucifixion, Jesus still was not transformed totally and permanently into the fourth dimensional frequency body. Even after the crucifixion he needed time to adjust to that higher, etheric frequency. For he said to Mary of Magdala on that Easter morn, "Touch me not, for I have not yet ascended unto my Father." He did not ascend for another forty days.

Why was that cautionary measure necessary? Mary of Magdala represents that aspect of the soul which, having sinned and being bedeviled with error conditions, is willing and able to be transformed. She is capable of full repentance (turning around from error to truth) when consciously touched by the Christ. If Jesus himself, even after resurrecting the individualized self in a new form, still had to transmute some of the old mortal threads hanging on to his personality, the rest of us should not be discouraged when we too have to transmute Earth-type thoughts, words, actions and relationships.

There still will be such times for elimination, renunciation, denial when in the I Am consciousness. No matter in what society, environment, dimension or plane of activity we are having experiences and are performing responsibilities, we are vulnerable to a certain amount of debris and pollution. The angelic forces, as well as members of the race of man, must be alert to such inevitable conditions. How do we rid ourselves of them? We bathe ourselves in the brilliant, all-consuming violet flame, thereby transmuting mind, soul and physical form.

196

PHYSICAL DATA
Urinary System & Colon

The spiritual quality of elimination–renunciation–denial outpictures via the sacral chakra as the urinary system and the colon. The urinary system—consisting of two kidneys, two ureters, the bladder and the urethra—filters the blood and excretes urine. (See Figure 12a.) The colon or large intestine removes wastes, such as roughage, that are left over from digestion. (See Figure 12b.)

Urinary System. Every cell in the body produces metabolic by-products that diffuse into the blood, which carries them to the two kidneys. Shaped like lima beans, the kidneys are located laterally to the spinal column in the low back area. In addition to removing metabolic

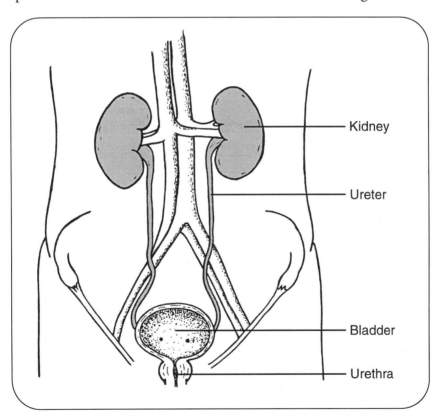

Figure 12a. Urinary system (male).

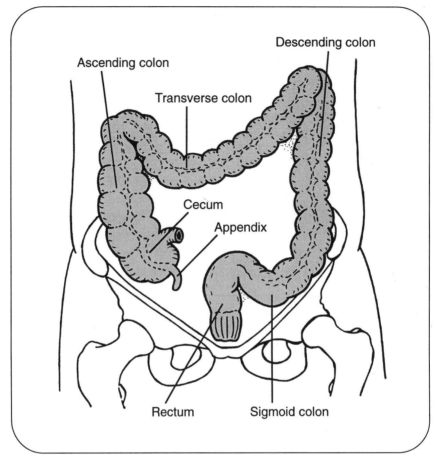

Figure 12b. Colon (shaded).

wastes such as urea and uric acid from the blood, the kidneys also filter out excess water and minerals, bacterial toxins, degraded hormones, toxic chemicals and other unneeded substances. However, red and white blood cells, platelets, needed minerals, proteins and other nutrients are retained in the blood.

The filtering of the blood by the kidneys produces urine, which is approximately ninety-five percent water and five percent solutes. Urine travels down through the ten-to-twelve-inch-long ureters to the bladder, which is a muscular sac capable of extension. During urination, the urinary sphincters open and the bladder muscles contract, thereby expelling urine through the urethra to outside the body.

198

Colon. The colon also is called the large intestine because its average diameter of two and one-half inches is larger than the diameter of the small intestine. The colon consists of the cecum, the ascending colon, the transverse colon, the descending colon, the sigmoid colon, the rectum and the anus. Projecting from the cecum is a finger-shaped organ, the appendix, which averages three to four inches in length. It contains a large amount of lymphoid tissue.

Undigested food (including roughage or fiber), water, mineral salts, pigments and some toxic items move into the colon through the ileocecal valve, which is located between the end of the ileum (last section of the small intestine) and the first part of the colon, the cecum. Most of the water and the mineral salts are reabsorbed in the ascending colon and the first half of the transverse colon. This leads to the solidification of the waste matter or feces, which are stored in the second half of the transverse colon, the descending colon and the sigmoid colon. During defecation, the feces are removed via the rectum and out the anus.

Other organs have minor eliminatory functions. The lungs have fine hairs, called cilia, lining their airways to catch dust and other particles, which then are swept upward and can be coughed out of the system. The skin releases small amounts of toxins through sweating. The liver, the spleen and the lymphatic system purify the blood. However, the urinary system and the colon remove most of the wastes and the toxins from the body. That is why they are the principal organs of elimination.

When we fail to renounce and to eliminate harmful habits, negative thoughts or feelings, or imbalanced soul patterns, we may develop disorders of the urinary system and the colon. Urinary diseases include infections of the urethra, the bladder or the kidneys; cysts and tumors (benign and malignant) of the bladder and the kidney; and kidney stones. Colon disorders may produce symptoms such as constipation and diarrhea. Common colon diseases include spastic or irritable colon, Crohn's colitis, ulcerative colitis, diverticulosis and diverticulitis, appendicitis, and polyps and cancer of the colon.

COLOR VISUALIZATION
Violet

The violet flame is an all-consuming fire which is not hot. It is comfortable. It is desirable to be in it. Deliberately rise into the I Am state of consciousness. Then visualize a violet flame at least two feet in front of the physical body. Place yourself in it with a sense of joy and expectancy; knowing it cannot harm, but only can help spiritually. From the third eye, look before you at your own aura. See it also encased by this beautiful flame of nonburning fire. Remember, the aura is the envelope around the physical body, and comprises all mental, emotional and soul-psychic patterns. It not only surrounds the physical sac but it influences all of its functions.

Visualize all levels of your being as cleansed in this violet flame. If there is any condition, person or situation limiting full I Am Self externalization, renounce its connections to your body and auric envelope. Burn off the ties that bind you to mortal ways and thinking and which prevent the fullness of the I Am Self from expressing. One by one, and in different meditation sessions, place into the violet flame friends, relatives, soul patterns, limiting codes and philosophies, troubling dreams, memories of past failures. Burn off all threads impeding your progress. Properly motivated and activated this way, the violet flame harms no one, nothing. But it sets you free.

Feelings and emotions, ideas and customs, associations and relationships, physical limitations and errors are eliminated, renounced, denied. They disappear. This is your rightful duty, one of the twelve characteristics of the I Am Self.

According to the results that manifest in your life and affairs, you are able to discern for yourself just how successful you are in flexing that function of the I Am Self. But if you should fall short of the mark, repeat the visualization with the violet flame of transmutation.

In time, when the aura appears as pure gold, you will know all dross has been burned away. The golden aura is a reflection of your light body, the Godness of your efforts. The I Am Self is fully operative as an independent individualization within the Christ body of mankind. You are home, free!

SONG INSPIRATION
Elimination

Been doing the same things life after life;
I've done it before, but it wasn't so right.
The same kind of people still knock on my door,
But soon they won't find me here anymore.

200

Packing my bags, gonna let go,
Leaving the things I don't need anymore.
It's the final step on a long, long road.
Finishing up, it's time to go.

Saying good-bye to nasty habits,
Bidding *adieu* to all that's untrue,
Adiós to my old *amigos*,
Arrivederci, I'm starting anew.
I'll be flying high and moving free,
'Cos one with God is the way to be.
With nothing to bind me and nothing to lose,
Ain't singing the transmutation blues.

I've canceled my ticket for the wrong destination.
I'm burning the bridges to the land of temptation.
I've found the path that's narrow and straight.
I'm changing my ways before it's too late.
I've seen the way I want to be.
I've seen the light inside of me.
I'm ready to surrender, ready to release,
Eliminate the thoughts that rob me of my peace.

Saying good-bye to nasty habits,
Bidding *adieu* to all that's untrue,
Adiós to my old *amigos*,
Arrivederci, I'm starting anew.
I'll be flying high and moving free,
'Cos one with God is the way to be.
With nothing to bind me I'm on my way.
I'm singing my freedom song today.
I'm singing my freedom song today.

SONG INSPIRATION
I Am Golden Light

I am golden light.
I am love in action.
Linking and uniting,
This is my demonstration.

We are golden light.
We are love in action.
Linking and uniting,
We are the I Am Nation.

I am faith and strength united.
I am love and I am wise.
I do God's will with God's own power,
Golden light to spiritualize.

Through my clear window I see visions
Of a world that understands
The importance of our mission,
The importance of God's plan.

All things balanced with new order,
Bringing forth a greater zeal.
New life for each one wholly,
Saving only what is real.

We are golden light.
We are love in action.
Linking and uniting,
This is our demonstration.

You are golden light.
You are love in action.
Linking and uniting,
You are the I Am Nation.

GLOSSARY
Names & New Age Terms

akashic record: soul history of an individual, a race, a heavenly body.

angel: a being of celestial realms.

Aquarian Age: period of approximately two thousand years following the Piscean Age. Cycle during which the solar system moves through the area of cosmic space known as Aquarius.

archangel: head of a ray of life in this solar system. First: Michael. Second: Jophiel. Third: Chamuel (replaced Lucifer). Fourth: Gabriel. Fifth: Raphael. Sixth: Zadkiel. Seventh: Uriel.

Armageddon: the Latter-Day, cleansing, harvest, Mark Age period immediately prior to the Second Coming of Sananda as Christ Jesus. The era wherein man must eliminate the negativity in himself and the world.

ascended master: one who has reached the Christ level and who has translated his or her physical body into the light body or etheric body.

ascension: spiritual initiation and achievement wherein one translates the physical body into a higher dimension.

astral: pertaining to realms or planes between physical and etheric. Lower astral realms approximate Earth plane level of consciousness; higher astral realms approach etheric or Christ realms.

astral body: one of the seven bodies of man pertaining to Earth plane life. Appearance is similar to physical body. Upon transition called death it becomes the operative body for the consciousness, in the astral realms.

Atlantis: civilization springing from Lemuria, dating from 206,000 to 10,000 years ago. Land area was from present eastern part of USA and the Caribbean to western part of Europe, but not all one land mass. Sinking of Atlantis was from 26,000 to 10,000 years ago; allegory of Noah and the Flood.

at-onement: conscious unification.

aura: the force field around an object, especially a person. Contains information graphically revealed in color to those able to see with spiritual vision.

auric: pertaining to the aura.

automatic writing: a channeled communication by one from another realm written via control of the subconscious of the channel or instrument over the hands. May be handwritten or typewritten. Paintings or drawings can be done via such automatic process.

bilocation: being in more than one place at the same time.

cause and effect, law of: as you sow, so shall you reap.

celestial: angelic.

chakra: a center of energy focus, generally located around one of the seven major endocrine glands, but which penetrates the other, more subtle, bodies.

channel: a person who is used to transmit communications, energies, thoughts, deeds by either Spirit or an agent of Spirit. Also called prophet, sensitive, recorder, medium, instrument.

children of God: the race of man.

chohans: directors of the Seven Rays of Life, under the archangels. First: El Morya. Second: Kut Humi. Third: Lanto. Fourth: Serapis Bey. Fifth: Hilarion. Sixth: St. Germain. Seventh: Sananda with Nada. As channeled through Yolanda numerous times.

Christ: a title indicating achievement of the spiritual consciousness of a son of God. Also refers to the entire race of man as and when operating in that level of consciousness.

Christ, anti-: one who does not accept brotherhood and equality of all men as sons of God.

Christ awareness: awareness of the Christ level within one's self and of the potential to achieve such.

Christ consciousness: achievement of some degree of understanding and use of spiritual powers and talents.

Christ Self: the superconscious, I Am, higher Self, oversoul level of consciousness.

clairaudience: ability to hear above the physical level or range of sound on Earth. A spiritual talent.

clairvoyance: ability to see beyond the physical range of vision; seeing via the third eye. A spiritual talent.

conscious mind: the mortal level of one's total consciousness; which is about one tenth of such total consciousness. Usually refers to the rational, thinking aspect in man.

consciousness, mass: collective consciousness of race of man on Earth, all planes or realms pertaining to Earth.

Creative Energy: a designation for God or Spirit or Creative Force.

death: transition from physical life or expression on Earth to another realm, such as physical incarnation on some other planet or expression on astral or etheric realms.

dematerialize: change of rate of frequency vibration so as to disappear from third dimensional range of Earth plane sensing.

devas: those intelligent entities of the etheric planes who control the patterns for manifested form in the etheric, Earth and astral planes, under the direction of the angelic kingdom.

devic: one of the kingdoms of God's creation of entities; see *devas*.

dimension: a plane or realm of manifestation. A range of frequency vibration expression, such as third dimensional physical on Earth.

disease: condition of dis-ease or disharmony.

Divine Mind: God or Spirit; in reality the only mind that exists, man having a consciousness within this one mind.

Elder race: those sons of God who did not become entrapped in the third dimension as the human subrace.

elect: one who has been chosen by Spirit and the Hierarchal Board to participate in the hierarchal plan and program, and who had elected so to be chosen. One of the symbolic 144,000 demonstrators and teachers for this spiritual program.

elementals: those intelligent entities supervising the elements which comprise manifested form in the Earth and astral planes, under the direction of the devas for those forms.

El Morya Khan: Chohan of First Ray. Prince of Neptune. El denotes Spirit and the Elder race. Morya is a code scrambling of Om Ray. Khan is a Sanskrit term meaning king. No Earth incarnation since Atlantis (despite claims by others), until as Mark Age or Charles Boyd Gentzel (1922–1981), a cofounder and director of Mark-Age.

elohim: one or more of the seven elohim in the Godhead, heading the Seven Rays of Life; creators of manifestation for Spirit.

emotional body: one of the seven bodies of man pertaining to Earth life. Does not in any way resemble the physical body, but has the connotation of a vehicle for expression.

ESP: elementary spiritual powers, the definition coined by Mark-Age in 1966 to supersede the limited and nonspiritual usual meaning as extrasensory perception.

etheric: the Christ realms. Interpenetrates the entire solar system, including the physical and astral realms.

etheric body: one of the seven bodies of man pertaining to Earth life. Known more commonly as the light body, the electric body, the resurrected body, the ascended body. Resembles the physical body, but not necessarily of the same appearance. This body can be used by the Christ Self for full expression of Christ talents and powers.

eye, third: the spiritual sight or vision. Spiritual focus of light in center of forehead.

fall of man: sons of God becoming entrapped in the third or physical dimension of Earth from 206,000,000 to 26,000,000 years ago.

Father-Mother God: indicates male-female or positive-negative principle and polarities of Spirit. Also, Father denotes action and ideation, while Mother symbolizes receptive principles.

Father-Mother-Son: the Holy Trinity wherein Father is originator of idea for manifestation, Mother (Holy Spirit or Holy Ghost) brings forth the idea into manifestation, Son is the manifestation. Son also denotes the Christ or the race of mankind, universally.

Federation of Planets: coordination and cooperation of man on all planets of this solar system, except as yet man of physical and astral realms of Earth.

Fillmore, Charles: (1854–1948) cofounder of metaphysical Unity School of Christianity, now located in Unity Village, Missouri. Last Earth incarnation of Hilarion.

forces, negative: individuals, groups or forces not spiritually enlightened or oriented, but who think and act in antispiritual manners.

fourth dimension: in spiritual sense, the next phase of Earthman's evolution into Christ awareness and use of ESP, elementary spiritual powers. In physical sense, the next higher frequency vibration range into which Earth is being transmuted.

free will: man's divine heritage to make his own decisions. Pertains fully only to the Christ Self; and only in part and for a limited, although often lengthy, period to the mortal self or consciousness during the soul evolvement.

frequency vibration: a range of energy expressing as matter. Present Earth understanding and measurement, as in cycles per second, not applicable.

gift of tongues: thought transference, in actuality, via speaking of unknown languages.

Golden Age or Era: the coming New Age or Aquarian Age, taking effect with the return of Sananda around the end of the twentieth century. It will be the age of greatest spiritual enlightenment in Earth's history.

guide: higher plane teacher for one still on the Earth plane.

heaven: an attitude and atmosphere of man's expression, wherever he is. No such specific place, as believed by some religions; except to denote the etheric realms.

hell: an attitude and atmosphere of man's expression, wherever he is. No such specific place, as believed by some religions.

Hierarchal Board: the spiritual governing body of this solar system. Headquarters is on Saturn.

hierarchal plan and program: the 26,000-year program ending by the year 2000 A.D. wherein the Hierarchal Board has been lifting man of Earth into Christ awareness preparatory to the manifestation of spiritual government on Earth and the return of Earth to the Federation of Planets of this solar system.

Hierarchy, spiritual: the spiritual government of the solar system, from the Hierarchal Board down through the individual planetary departments.

Hilarion: Chohan of Fifth Ray. Last Earth incarnation was as Charles Fillmore (1854–1948), cofounder of Unity School of Christianity. Other Earth incarnations have been as Plato the philosopher and as Paul the Apostle for Christ Jesus of Nazareth.

I Am: the Christ or high Self of each person. Yahweh (Jehovah), in the Old Testament. Atman or Brahman.

I Am Nation: spiritual government of, for and by the I Am Selves of all people on Earth, to be inaugurated officially by Sananda upon his Second Coming. Neither a religion nor a political government, it is the congregation of all souls dedicated, above any other allegiance, to God and to expressing the I Am Self. Regardless of race, gender, age, nationality, religion or esoteric group affiliation, everyone is a potential I Am Nation citizen. On May 10, 1974, the Hierarchal Board commissioned Mark-Age to implant the prototype of the I Am Nation.

I am that I Am: identification of the Christ Self with God.

incarnation: one lifetime of a soul; not always referring to an experience on Earth only.

Jesus of Nazareth: last Earth incarnation of Sananda. Christ Jesus, rather than Jesus Christ; for Christ is not a name but is a level of spiritual attainment which all mankind will reach and which many already have attained.

John the Beloved: disciple of Christ Jesus; author of Gospel of John and of Revelation in the New Testament. An incarnation of Kut Humi, Chohan of Second Ray.

karma: that which befalls an individual because of prior thoughts and deeds, in this or former lifetimes. Can be good or bad, positive or negative.

karma, law of: otherwise known as law of cause and effect. What one sows, so shall he reap.

Karmic Board: that department of the spiritual Hierarchy of this solar system which reviews and passes on each individual's soul or akashic record. Assigns or permits incarnations, lessons, roles, missions for everyone in this solar system.

karmic debt: that which one owes payment for, due to action in this or prior lifetimes. Must be paid off at some time in a spiritually proper manner.

kingdoms: celestial, man, animal, vegetable, mineral, devic. Denotes a category of divine creation. Evolution is only within the same kingdom, never through the various kingdoms. Transmigration—incarnation of an entity in different kingdoms—is an invalid theory.

kundalini: spiritual force which rises up through the spine in the process of awakening the mortal personality to the spiritual consciousness and powers. Symbolically called the snake or serpent. The fire of the kundalini begins in the lower spine or sex center (chakra), rising gradually until reaching the head or crown chakra, where union takes place with the Christ Self.

language, universal sign: transmission of messages, commands, energies or stories through higher plane control of body movements, especially arms and hands, of a channel.

Lemuria: civilization dating from 26,000,000 to 10,000 years ago. Land area was from western USA out into Pacific Ocean. Final destruction was 10,000–13,000 years ago; allegory of Noah and the Flood.

levitation: lifting one's body off the ground by spiritual or by higher plane equipment means.

light: spiritual illumination; spiritual; etheric. Also, God as Light.

light body: fourth dimensional body of man; his etheric or Christ body; one of the seven bodies relating to Earth living; the resurrected or ascended body through which the Christ powers and talents can be demonstrated.

light worker: a spiritual worker in the hierarchal plan and program.

logos: a spiritual entity manifesting a stellar or a planetary body, such as a solar logos or a planetary logos.

Lord: God; laws of God; spiritual title for officeholder in Hierarchy; designation given to one who has mastered all laws of a specified realm.

Love God and Love One Another: the two laws which Christ Jesus gave unto man of Earth. The motto of the White Brotherhood, the light workers in this solar system.

Love In Action: the New Age teaching of action with high Self, action with love; the Mark-Age theme and motto.

Mark Age: designation of the Latter-Day period, when there are appearing signs of the times to demonstrate the ending of the old age. Also, designation for the Earth plane aspect of the hierarchal plan. Also, the spiritual name for El Morya in his incarnation on Earth as Charles Boyd Gentzel (1922–1981), cofounder of Mark-Age unit.

Mark-Age: with the hyphen, designates the unit cofounded in 1960 by incarnated Hierarchal Board members El Morya (Charles Boyd Gentzel) and Nada (Yolanda of the Sun, or Pauline Sharpe). One of many focal points on Earth for the Hierarchal Board. Coordination Unit #7 and initial focus for externalization of the Hierarchal Board on Earth in the Latter Days.

Mary the Mother: mother of Sananda when he last incarnated on Earth, as Jesus of Nazareth. Twin soul of Sananda. Her Earth incarnations include those as Zolanda, a high priestess in Atlantis; and as King Solomon, son of David, mentioned in the Old Testament.

master: one who has mastered something. An ascended master is one who has achieved Christhood and has translated or has raised his or her physical body to the fourth dimension.

master ship #10: mother-ship spacecraft of city size which is Sananda's headquarters for the Mark Age period and program. Has been in etheric orbit around Earth since about 1885. Will be seen by those on Earth when time approaches for Sananda's return to Earth as Christ Jesus of Nazareth and as Sananda, Prince of Earth.

materialization: coupled with dematerialization. Mat and demat are a transmutation or translation from one frequency vibration to another, from one plane or realm to another. Translation of chemical, electronic and auric fields of an individual or object.

Matthias: an incarnation of St. Germain, Chohan of Sixth Ray; the replacement for Judas among the disciples of Jesus.

meditation: spiritual contemplation to receive illumination, or to experience at-onement with Spirit or one's own Christ Self or another agent of Spirit, or to pray or to decree or to visualize desired results.

mental body: one of the seven bodies of man pertaining to Earth living. Does not look like a physical body.

metaphysics: spiritual meaning is the study of that which lies beyond the physical, of the basic spiritual laws of the universe, and the practical application thereof in daily life on Earth.

miracle: a spiritual manifestation, or a work. There are no so-called miracles possible, in the sense of circumventing a divine law.

mortal consciousness: the awareness of a soul during Earth incarnation, prior to Christ consciousness.

Nada: Co-Chohan, with Sananda, of Seventh Ray. Member of Karmic Board of Hierarchal Board. Present Earth incarnation is as Yolanda of the Sun, or Pauline Sharpe, primary channel and executive director of Mark-Age.

negative polarity: refers to the female principle in creation. The rest or passive nature, as complementing the positive or action polarity.

New Age: the incoming Golden Age or Aquarian Age. Actually began entry about 1960.

New JerUSAlem: the United States of America will become the spiritual pattern for implementing spiritual government on Earth in the coming Golden Age.

Om; or Aum: a designation for God. Means power.

one hundred and forty-four thousand: the elect, the demonstrators and the teachers of Christ powers during the Mark Age period and program. The number is literal, in that at least that number must so demonstrate to achieve the spiritual goal of lifting man into the fourth dimension, and symbolic, in that it does not preclude any number of additional ones from being included.

physical body: one of the seven bodies of man for living on Earth. Has been expressing in third dimension, but will be well into the fourth dimension by end of twentieth century. The vehicle for mortal expression of the soul on Earth. The physical on other planets of our solar system expresses as high as the eighth dimension.

plane: a realm, a dimension, a level of expression.

positive polarity: the male or action focus, as complementing the negative or female or passive polarity.

prince: a spiritual office and title, such as Sananda being Prince of Love and Peace as Chohan of Seventh Ray, and Prince of Earth as spiritual ruler of this planet.

prophet: in addition to usual meaning it is the term preferred by those of higher planes in referring to a communications channel.

psychic: refers to the powers of man focused through the solar plexus chakra or center. Not as high as the Christ powers.

realm: plane, dimension, a level of expression.

reincarnation: taking on another incarnation, on any plane or planet, during one's eternal life.

Sananda: Chohan of Seventh Ray. Prince or spiritual ruler of Earth. One of Council of Seven, highest ruling body of the solar system. Previous Earth incarnations: Christ Jesus of Nazareth, his last one; biblical Melchizedek, Moses and Elijah; Zarathustra; Gautama Buddha; Socrates, Greek philosopher; leader of Abels, in allegorical story of Cain and Abel; leader of Noahs, in allegorical story of Noah and the ark. Presently located in etheric realm, from whence he directs entire operation for upliftment of man and his own Second Coming; headquarters is master ship #10, in etheric orbit around Earth since about 1885.

Saturnian Council: Council of Seven, highest ruling body of the solar system. Headquarters is on planet Saturn.

Second Coming: refers to each coming into awareness of his or her own Christ Self, and the return of Sananda as Jesus of Nazareth to institute spiritual government on Earth by 2000 A.D.

Self, high: Christ Self, I Am presence, superconscious, oversoul, Atman, Yahweh (Jehovah). The spiritual Self of each individual. Differentiated, in writing, from mortal self by use of capital *S* in Self.

self, mortal: the spiritually unawakened consciousness of Earthman.

sensitive: a channel, prophet, instrument, medium. One who is sensitive to or aware of spiritual realms and occupants therein.

Seven Rays of Life: the seven major groupings of aspects of God; the seven flames. First: will and power (blue). Second: intelligence and wisdom (yellow). Third: personal love and feeling (pink). Fourth: crystallization (colorless, crystal-clear). Fifth: unity, integration, healing, balance (green). Sixth: transmutation, cleansing, purification (violet). Seventh: divine love, peace, rest (gold and white). As channeled numerous times by Yolanda.

sin, original: man's mistaken belief that he can have an existence away from or be separated from Spirit.

Son of God: with capital *S* for Son, denotes the Christ body of all mankind, collectively. With small *s* for son, denotes an individual. All men are sons of God and eventually will come into that awareness, heritage, power and co-creativity with God.

Son, only begotten: refers to the entire Christ body, which includes all of mankind, and not just a single individual.

soul: the accumulation of an individual's experiences in his or her eternal living. A covering or a coat of protection, over which the individual spirit can and does rely for its manifestations.

Source: a term for God, sometimes called Divine Source.

sphere: planet, realm, plane, dimension, level of expression.

Spirit: God, Creative Energy, Creative Force, Divine Mind, Father-Mother God, Original Source.

spirit: the spiritual consciousness or Self of man.

spiritual: term preferred over *religious* when referring to spiritual matters, as there are specific dogma and connotation attached to *religious.*

subconscious: one of the three phases of mind. Denotes the soul or record-keeper phase, which also performs the automatic and maintenance functions of the physical body. The relay phase between the superconscious and conscious aspects of one's total consciousness.

superconscious: the highest of the three aspects of individual consciousness, consisting also of conscious and subconscious aspects. The Christ, I Am, real, high Self. The real individual, which projects into embodiment via having created a physical body for such incarnation.

sword of truth: denotes the use of God's word and law to eliminate error, and to guide and to protect spiritual persons.

teleportation: spiritual power enabling one to move from one location to another via dematerialization and materialization, without physical means. A Christ power. Symbol for this in Atlantis was dodo bird.

tests, spiritual: tests of one's spiritual progress and lessons learned, given by Spirit, by one's own Christ Self or by other spiritual teachers. Not temptings, which never are given anyone by any of the above guides.

third dimension: the frequency vibrational level in which Earth and all on it have been expressing physically for eons. Being transmuted into the fourth dimension, which was begun gradually by the mid-twentieth century for completion in the twenty-first century, but well into the process by the end of the twentieth. Does not refer to the three dimensions of length, width and height, but to a range of vibration.

thought form: an actual form beyond the third dimension, created by man's thoughts. Has substance in another plane and can take on limited powers and activities, based on the power man has instilled in it through his thoughts and beliefs.

transfiguration: a change of one's features, or of entire body, caused by overshadowing by one's Christ Self or by an ascended master.

transition: term denoting death of an individual on one plane so as to begin a new life on another plane. Also, general meaning of making a change.

transmutation: spiritually, refers to purifying one's mortal consciousness and body so as to permit raising into fourth dimension, physically and as concerns Christ consciousness.

trials: spiritual tests given one in evolution to see if lessons are learned or if obstacles can be overcome, as in training for a soul mission.

Trinity, Holy: Father-Mother-Son, Father-Holy Spirit-Son, Father-Holy Ghost-Son. The three aspects of God.

twenty-six-million-year cycle: a period of evolution for man in this solar system. The cycle since the final fall of man on Earth, during which the Elder race has been attempting to raise the human race that had become entrapped in the third dimension. Cycle to end 2000 A.D.

twenty-six-thousand-year cycle: the period of time, since the beginning of the fall of Atlantis, in which man of Earth has been given the last opportunity in this solar system for reevolution into the fourth dimension. Duration of a hierarchal plan and program to raise man from the third dimension into true status as sons of God. Cycle to end 2000 A.D.

two-hundred-and-six-million-year cycle: an evolutionary cycle for man involving graduation in and around the central sun from which we originated. The period during which man has experimented with life form on Earth in the third dimension. Cycle to end 2000 A.D.

two-hundred-and-six-thousand-year cycle: withdrawal of the Elder race from on Earth, and decline of Lemuria. Cycle to end 2000 A.D.

vehicle: denotes the body for one's expression, such as physical body.

veil, seventh: final veil separating man from knowing his divine heritage and powers.

vibrations: the frequency range in which something is expressing; not in terms of cycles per second, or any present Earth understanding and terminology. Also, the radiations emitted by an individual, able to be received consciously by one spiritually sensitive to such emanations.

world, end of: denotes ending of third dimensional expression for Earth and all on it, physically, and entry into a higher level of frequency vibration, the fourth dimension. The end of the materially-minded world of man so as to begin spiritual understanding and evolvement. Does not mean end of the Earth, but only entering a higher dimension.

Yahweh (Jehovah): biblical term for Christ or I Am Self.

Yolanda of the Sun: present Earth incarnation of Nada as Pauline Sharpe, executive director of Mark-Age. Was her name at height of her Atlantean development, when a high priestess of the Sun Temple, located near what is now Miami, Florida. Also known as Yolanda of the Temple of Love on the etheric realm of Venus.

MARK-AGE

Mastership Books

HOW TO DO ALL THINGS. Your use of divine power. Achieve union with your inner Self & master your life. Demonstrate your true heritage & powers as a child of God. By El Morya/Mark. **$8**

EVOLUTION OF MAN. Origin, history, destiny of man. Major evolutionary cycles of Earthman in past 206 million years. Nature & powers of I Am consciousness. Channeled via Nada-Yolanda. **$15**

ANGELS & MAN. Seven archangels reveal nature & function of angels, unveiling cosmic relationship with & guardianship of man. Sequel to *Evolution of Man*. Channeled via Nada-Yolanda. **$15**

1000 KEYS TO THE TRUTH. Guidelines for Latter Days, Second Coming, mastership, karma, reincarnation, spiritual space program, healing, more. Based on channelings of Nada-Yolanda. **$7**

MAPP* TO AQUARIUS: *Mark Age Period & Program. Navigate the New Age with a tested road map for these Latter Days prior to Second Coming. Channeled via Nada-Yolanda. **$15**

VISITORS FROM OTHER PLANETS. Who they are & why they are here to assist our spiritual evolution into New Age. Federation of Planets. Mass landings. Channeled via Nada-Yolanda. **$15**

MARK-AGE · P.O. Box 290368
FT. LAUDERDALE, FL 33329, USA

Life Production Company presents . . .

I AM GOLDEN LIGHT

by Light Wave

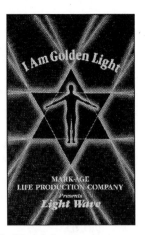

Twelve qualities of our I Am Self vibrate to life through the dynamic harmonies of this spiritually inspired cassette. Each of the songs (arranged in a wide variety of music styles and settings) focuses on one divine power or quality. The twelve powers unfold as we anchor the light body, the fourth dimensional or resurrected form of our I Am Self. Christ Jesus demonstrated the light body after his resurrection; others of all spiritual paths likewise have expressed their light body and Christ talents.

With vibrational power, these songs evoke and uplift each quality and its corresponding chakra center and physical system. Songs include: Faith, Strength, Love, Wisdom, Will, Power, Imagination, Understanding, Order, Zeal, Regeneration, Elimination, and I Am Golden Light.

I Am Golden Light was inspired by teachings of the light body and the twelve spiritual systems as given in the Mark-Age text *Birth of the Light Body* by Nada-Yolanda, primary channel and executive director, with scientific-medical data by Robert H. Knapp, M.D., director of Healing Haven. To order, send $11 to:

Mark-Age, Inc. · P.O. Box 290368 · Ft. Lauderdale, FL 33329, USA

left to right:
Janet Thiemermann
Deborah Jacobs